TWISTS AND TURNS IN THE HEART'S ANTARCTIC

TWISTS AND TURNS IN THE HEART'S ANTARCTIC

HÉLÈNE CIXOUS

TRANSLATED BY BEVERLEY BIE BRAHIC

polity

First published in French as *Revirements dans l'antarctique du coeur*
© Éditions Galilée, 2011

This English edition © Polity Press, 2014

Polity Press
65 Bridge Street
Cambridge CB2 1UR, UK

Polity Press
350 Main Street
Malden, MA 02148, USA

ISBN-13: 978-0-7456-6327-2
ISBN-13: 978-0-7456-6328-9 (pb)

A catalogue record for this book is available from the British Library.

Typeset in 10.75 on 14 pt Janson Text by
Servis Filmsetting Ltd, Stockport, Cheshire
Printed and bound by Clays Ltd, St Ives plc

For further information on Polity, visit our website: www.politybooks.com

CONTENTS

v

Part III

AUTHOR'S PREFACE

The family is destroying itself.
– There's a body in the middle of the dining room, the Sister says. – No, says the Brother.
– There's a body, I said. You can't say this, it's the thing you aren't supposed to say. This is the meaning of *Family*: there are never any dead bodies in the dining room. It was me who said it. In the family, my role is to say things. I should add that I was expecting something of the sort. On the one hand, we had a death in the family. O. and I engendered it during a furious argument. On the other hand, never had an entire firmament burned as brightly and as steadily in mama. This dead body, I told myself, is us . . . But I'm the only one who thinks this.

With love's strength, one hates. "You hate me! You hate me!" one shouts in a frenzy of delight, and one really and truly feels that one hates the hate as if it were love. One is hateloved with hate, one is contaminated. And a brother says: "No." One wants to hate in hiding, burn without a torch.

In the fusion between literature and life, I'd written a play for the Great Theater. Then I'd left the play behind. It lived on, on the other continent. In the scene called "Mayerling or the Most Violent Dispute" the Archduke cries: "You hate me You want me dead." But a voice mingles with the despairing voice. It's the Voice of his father, the Archduke's father. One hears him – him too – shout: "You want me dead." One doesn't see the Emperor. The scene is full of Voices. The horror of being torn apart by the person one loves is in itself a death added to death. One doesn't see the father howl but his cries are reproduced, exactly, by the son.

Suddenly a shot rings out. The Archduke is dead. Bang. Could that have been my brother?

"If you could kill me, you'd do it right here right now!" I thought. "Shut up," I told my thought. But it got though all the same. Death has the power to turn itself into us. When it comes along, nothing in the world can stop it. Already I saw the scene. There was, in the house where these exceptionally violent events were taking place, on a shelf or in one of my bags, the text of the play I'd written for the Great Theater and thus, without my being in the least aware of this, the scenario of a scene whose theme and dialogues are practically the doubles of the violent dispute. It came to me that the play had entered my soul more deeply than I could have imagined. Other thoughts came to me.

There was a gun too.

"So long as I live you won't write," O. gave me to understand, in his language, the language of doors slamming, smashed porcelain. Now O. openly led the charge against H. to keep her from writing, O. set off explosives on the staircase fireplace. Basalt vomit.

O. follows me onto the staircase. He aims his gun. Meanwhile I stalk O. from within. Since one dimly feels that the ties of clan are by definition unbreakable, on the one hand one can ramp up the violence, on the other one has a desperate desire to let oneself go, in line with the impossibility of breaking blood ties. These invisible ties are the most frequent causes of murders.

If I've forgotten that I really used to be an author-of-plays, it's because I have fallen from the theater's heights. I am an angel bereft of her dreams. Aloft in the clouds, I woke myself with my cries from below, my earth cries. I was crying: "*I am going to kill myself or you are going to kill me,*" and this was not in the play I had written. Now I am in the play I didn't write, and in which I am being acted by the other characters, I can't leave the play, I can't want to leave it before the last act.

"I want to be alone, in my house, which is a book full of books," this is what I want absolutely to tell O., I want to declare my solitude to him, my malady, my book, my journey, I want absolutely to proclaim my silence to his noise. Naturally, one can't tell people: "Go away. I'm writing." Implacable are hospitality's laws, in the end the person who prefers to write is condemned to offer his coat to the neighbor, to allow him deeper and deeper into the house, to give a kiss to the plague. I can't say to O. "Don't be O." And what if I said it?

That's when I heard the door bang, then the words: "I'm leaving!" As if the door itself had shouted: *I'M LEAVING! BANG! LEAVING!* Everything is in the *B*!

There was a shot on the staircase. *Bang!* One is pierced by the bullet before one perceives the shot. It had already gone off.

– What's that noise? my mother asked, waving a bean in the air.

– O. left.

Still, hardly had O. left, hardly was O. on his way out the door, already, taking him to the station, I felt a real chagrin take O.'s place. One thinks one has got to the bottom of one's heart, this is an error. Another heart beats differently behind the heart's false ceiling. All of us are children, I tell myself. The feeling that O. is six years old. My mother too. Come back, O.!

   Twists and turns. Everything twists and turns.

PART I

O. Announces the Murder

We won't go to Montaigne, I was thinking during the voyage, the whole way I held my mother in my arms, like life itself so incomprehensibly strong whereas it is frail, and at the very moment I let such a sentence come to me, the car, a ship of the road, was heading south, toward the continent of Montaigne, the Montaigne paradise, we have set sail I was telling myself and at the same moment I saw Montaigne and I saw the sentence telling me *we won't go to Montaigne*, I was telling myself lovingly I would hold mama in my arms during this journey, I didn't hear it I saw it flutter so frail and so tenacious and settle on the first leaf I would find when we reached the house, for a voyage a thought of non-voyage, I thought, it's as exasperating as a sentence that refuses to launch a book. An annoying thought, I fought against it, but feebly – all my thoughts were for mama, except that one, I held her taking care not to hurt her for at the least pressure she cries out, one must handle her with abnormal delicacy, she is not the same species – I tried rather to run away from

3

it, it too suffered from a certain weakness, all the more remarkable as no name in the world is more powerful than Montaigne – aside from "mama" naturally – over time it has acquired the adamantine brilliance of a Moses, for example, I say "Montaigne" and all the people of literature start up – "Montaigne" and here come all the companions of my Other Voyage gathering their baggage, it is upon reaching the banks of the broad river with its tarnished gold waters that the vision of literature's people came to me, a single nation, I thought – we had passed that inland sea asleep under its stone bridges as under rigid and heavy horsemen whereas my mother, brittle and worn out as she may be, is as supple as a wave, and with a single inflexion of our rapid vehicle we veered west, and left Montaigne to rise in the east on its immortal encampment. – What's wrong? asked my mother. – All's well I said. I had sighed. *About Montaigne I kept silent.* Now there's a sentence I could like: "About Montaigne I kept silent." Keeper of silences. My mother too, when she was mother, kept her silences. She has always known when not to speak.

The trip takes seven hours. Did I run away from my sentence for seven hours? There are hunts that take you beyond time to the verges of crime, right to the point of bloodshed, this summer I'm going to give my mother *The Legend of Saint-Julian the Hospitaller* to read, it's a trip that traverses death, a Go-Too-Far, from one violent act to the next until the violence expires in an exhalation of stems of old rose stems, hearts clothed in hundreds of petals of fading violet. "We're getting close," I say. And the sentence? Fading away. It's closer to paper, I noticed. It has lost its bite. I could begin to think about it as past. It has never been anything but a mute ghost. A ghost of a ghost. I have never said it aloud, it beat its wings against the walls and window panes, the way warnings of harm do. One must not name the temptations out loud, as

4

is said in Shakespeare. The minute a prediction is released into the air, the sky is poisoned, stars fall down, crowns roll in excrement. "Not long now," I rocked mama. Yet another sentence which taps several times on the glass: "Do you hear me?" she says. I pretend not to hear. I say: "Sixty kilometers left." This year I didn't go to India. I didn't go to the United States. I didn't go to Finland. This year is full of non-voyages. Voyages which could have happened, one prepared for them, one conjured them up, one gathered the supplies, one recruited the crew members, and the night before our departure, the possibility suddenly vanished. Not for this reason nor for that. Let's not talk about it. Instead of being in India, I was with mama, with mama I installed India on the couch in my study, this year I had mama for Finland, I couldn't look after mama without traversing the idea of Finland, then I traveled north of the Arctic Circle, on our way to the poles, mama complained of the cold, I draped her in sweaters and more sweaters, then I wrapped her in my dressing gown, we were laughing. – But what on earth is this cold? my mother would say. – It's the book, I said. She was reading *The Odyssey of "Endurance."* – Awful to be in the sea like that, surrounded by ice. Poor things. Says my mother.

We changed books. We took up *The Plague* and we went to Oran, the city of our childhood. And the cold came with us. – Poor old woman, said my mother. – Why do you say poor old woman? I ask. – When one is old one is poor. What can I give you? – A sentence, I say. – You want a sentence for today? How about: "I have no plans." I took the sentence my mother gave me. That's a beautiful strong sentence, I said. I watched it shine. I live by the light of mama's impoverishment, I tell myself. My mother's sentences are my arctic viaticum. She is snug in her boat whose name is *No.* Before my mother was a creature of plans. One loses the plans. Before Old Age my mother would travel with me. Since Old Age, she no longer

5

travels, I travel her, I take her in my arms, I sit her down on my inner divan, I couch her in my thoughts.

"I have no plans," my mother hummed.

Except to feel good

Good in my skin

I have no choice

The sun is shining, but

The Trapdoor is open

My mother is in her skin. We are in danger of getting stuck in the ice.

We are losing all our plans, it's like teeth, in the end, says my mother, I still have one tooth, I still have one plan, my entire voyage is in my skin, *the sun is shining, but*. I wrote that down in my blue notebook with the sailboats on it just before setting off with my mother in my arms, for real life. I note that I note: it's because we are losing. We are creatures who lack the strength to keep. This year I kept her noted, aware that we are by definition losers. Since I don't want to lose any of the illuminations I collect them in notebooks of different types and sizes. Then I forget where I put them. *The sun is shining, but/*the Trapdoor is open, the Sibyl says.

During the journey I don't look at the countryside, sometimes I look at my mother's face which offers a surface ravaged by weather, with crevices, lumps, cracks, her appearance changes every day, every day a work of inconceivable intensity is going on there, sometimes it looks to me like the majestic, inalterable image of Montaigne; the sun casts a shine on her skin that concedes nothing to age.

– What day is today? mama asked. The 26th of July? – Of June, my darling. I say "my darling" because she is. – I thought it was the 26th of July. – What happens on the 26th of July? I ask. My mother also travels in her ghostly realms. – Thatremindsme says my mother, back home, in Germany, on the 26th of July they were saying that there wouldn't be a war since it was my sister Éri's first birthday, someone said there will be war, a tone above it, my mother said there will not be a war, whereupon my father left, poor little Éri. A tiny little tear pearls in the corner of my mother's right eye, just one. This tear exercises its extraordinary power over me. It is a lamp in the ill-lit rooms where memory is kept, a sleeper now and then aroused by the light fingers of an association of thoughts. – Are you in 1914? I say to my mother. She'd just seen the whole legend of her sister in a single brilliant illumination, the fine day in July 1914 when the birthday didn't take place because they are removing the helmet and bayonet from the closet and right beside it, in the engraving crowded with lands and hills, the same day almost a hundred years later in which Éri was saying to her sister I want to go now, she wanted to go says my mother and she left. It's the 26th of June, for the entire journey my mother rides her century, her pale sister by her side. – We did a lot of traveling, says my mother. – We won't go to Montaigne again, buzzes the sentence. It has changed and it has returned, I note. Many other things have "changed." Let's not talk about them, what we talk about might come to pass.

There were pine trees. Then with its hands the sun opened the sky wide and waves of rose-colored light entered like a swarm of children, startling the cats: we have arrived. Thought the cats, my son and my mother. Not me, I thought, immediately.

I already *knew* and it's what I feared, and my fear was coming true all over the house, everywhere there were importunate forces, pressures, withdrawals of what makes the house my house, absence of homeyness, doors, which should have been closed gaped open, signs of negligence, traces of infinitesimal and thus perverse break-ins, and on my wide-open study door the notice on which I had years ago written by hand "study strictly personal, please do not enter" was weirdly upside down. "I am not in my skin" I thought, this is an extradition. I saw right away that for me there was no arrival, and not only saw. Didn't see the Peace, didn't hear the Silence, didn't find the household gods in their niches. Instead of not-a-sound, there is *Something Else*.

The storm hit the staircase. I am sure of it, I am shocked. There's a climate of war. Clatter of the regiment. Something infiltrating. It smells of *The Castle*. "You smell the castle? I say to my son. It smells of ash." But my son is too busy with the windmill. During the whole journey he talked about eolians, wings, mills. Me Tower, him Windmill. "This is the first time my study smells of Castle," I say to my son. I feel I'm mentally clutching at my son's helpful arm, his left arm, I put my right hand on his mental left hand, the scientist's artist's hand, his Leonardo da Vinci hand. – I'm cold, I say. We arrive and we see nothing, a kind of snow blankets everything. It's *the first time*, I say, and this ever since you were born of the house and in the house, never before upon arrival has there been no arrival, no peace, and snow everywhere and that it be invisible, like all the rest, which is the very characteristic of the Castle. – I don't see, says my son. – You see! What did I tell you! You don't see! –Mama! says my son, the astrophysicist. And to each his own anxiety.

When one arrives at the Castle, I say to my son who doesn't remember *The Castle*, on the one hand because he is fully occupied by his Windmill, on the other hand it is necessary to note because it is almost impossible to remember the Castle of *The Castle* distinctly, it is late in the evening, everything is invisible, the neighborhood is covered in snow, the hillside is deep in fog and shadows, one directs one's gaze toward the appearance of the invisible. "I see," says my son. But I don't feel it. And not only was I seeing the invisible appearance of everything that has always *made* the house, but I also felt forces of destruction gathering on the staircase. "I

8

feel," I say. Here I put my mother to bed. I saw everything in her room clearly. Next we spoke about dark matter. One doesn't see it, my son said, one is not at all sure that it exists. One really only detects its ghost. As we were in the dark, on the balcony, we didn't see. My son thought about George Green. I thought about Flaubert. Each allows his thoughts to come to him according to different temporal models.

"Flaubert died overnight," I say, "and no one was expecting it. Yet if there was one person who never stopped complaining about how poorly he was, it's him. I felt truly sorry," I say.

My son is looking at something below and ahead of him: Green's Windmill. I see that he sees. He inhales the wind's eddies deeply. In this precise moment, under these precise conditions, calm reigns. I *know* that it will be overthrown tomorrow. Dragged down the stairs. Executed. Don't tell. I'd noted in my little black travel diary: "That I'm still alive proves people don't die of sorrow." Such sadness to be still-living. Flaubert can't believe it. So he wrote to all his close friends. One isn't dead yet and one is only living still. That this idea of a life-still has infiltrated me in this past year is a cause for concern. *Infiltrated*, I say, because it hasn't invaded me. It's in me like my shadow. It doesn't go away, and while I look after my mother with the fierce and faultless attention of a mother, who carries on constant researches and reflections on death's share of the house, on the battles with their internal treacheries, on all the ills linked to our condition of being a regrafted recomposed mortgaged necessarily familied human being.

*

Maybe the Shadow is all the stronger as one comes to realize that truly *one doesn't die of sorrow.* Until the day when suddenly one does die of it. – I have no choice, says my mother. That's life. I am not sad, says my mother. I am poor. I am sad to be poor. It's not my fault. I am not guilty. I am doddery. I am do do do do doddery. The word doddery evokes a hoot of laughter. She is attracted to words that begin with do. But doddery transports her. Leave me the words! *Ich hab' doch sonst nichts.*

– Plume! I say, that's what you are.

From the window of my mother's room, I have a view of my life, that is, what stays in the window. It doesn't go very far. My mother doesn't move more than twenty meters in any direction. This circle's small dimensions are brightly lit by a perpetual inner starriness and by a collection of warm-hued flowers. We are in the red zone. Beyond and without transition is disaster. It's like a child's room. Before and in the old days it never occurred to me that I might become a mother at seventy. I saw myself dying in comfort as a poet one works like mad one devours oneself and one is devoured one inhabits braziers next the dead bring you bouquets of dreams, the house rustles all the way to the moon with telephoned messages, the cold increases with the fire, one stops counting the resurrections, and on average one makes one's exit from time in a handful of hours between fifty and sixty years of age. The unforeseen side of my story is my mother. The law that is not inscribed on the tablets of the law: thou shalt love the old infant as thyself. When one has an infant of this age, life is entirely a matter of submissions and emergencies, there isn't the least dark little corner into which a speck of the dust of ambivalence might seep. My mother's lack of power is the secret of her power.

My mother's room is all gold and sparkling laughter. Nothing could be simpler. The order is pure. No complaints. If I had something to reproach her with: that she prevents me taking flight. But I can't accuse her of this. I am in the countries beyond the moon where the *unknown* reigns supreme:

10

no one has ever been there. Everything needs to be invented. The names all work in this land, it's the referents that have changed. I say *read*. I give a *book* to my mother. She *reads*. This has absolutely nothing to do with any known way of "reading." It's another reading, I'll come back to this. No one *has ever read The Castle* (Kafka's) like my mother.

Let's take *a shower*. We proceed waveringly and with calculated hesitations. What looms up out of the bathroom mist is a smooth cliff whose side is shiny and falls off abruptly. – What do I do now? my mother asks. We halt at the tub's edge. It's a long narrow walk across a rock slippery with wet seaweed. My mother looks: I look: I see that she sees a dark green swell, a bit of uncontrolled tide whose look and temperature change *in a twinkling*. Too hot too cold too high too steep. – Turn around, I say. We seek the fault that offers the best foothold for her large worried foot. I am the ramp, I am the mast. Grab the towel rack, why don't you? One hoists the left foot. It is not very flexible, it is heavy, one raises it with a grunt, one lifts it to the edge, the water waits, my mother thinks about it, her foot dangles into the void, it looks for the ground. I am the ramp. Another few meters. Down. My mother consults me with a look – Next? – You lift the right leg, I say, Now we straddle a ridge. We pause. My mother catches her breath. With the strength of our arms I see we have scaled fifty meters. What an exploit this climb, elements of it are both attractive and frightening, and always the buzzing image of a fall that one swats off and which returns. One sits down for a long while. My mother cheeps. It's a victory all the same.

I am seated on the edge of the void. The water's mooing is the music of my thoughts. Flitting by on one wing a thought tosses "Where are my lives of yesteryear?" My eyes don't go after it. I have enough to do with this self that has come my way.

11

BANG!

– What's going on? my mother trembles.

What's banging I don't know quite how to describe, afterwards. Bang! Or bang, bang! The cats flee.

It's a shot. Or thunder. Or a door.

I think: it's O.

Banging the door isn't what he wanted. *BANG!* Another sound: this time it's a pile of dishes in the kitchen. Not what he wanted either. *GRR!* So? He'll kill the motor for good if he keeps his foot on the pedal. But it's something else, I tell myself, that O. wanted, it's something big, something Greek, with red filaments dribbling out of the corner of lips, and hoarse yells that roll around the trunk of the chest, the cadavers of slaughtered pets mounding over the scene's main cadaver, and the rasp of red anger, it's an action which responds on the one hand to a knot of threads whose uncontrollable tangle leads, without one being able to do anything about it, to a tragic moment, on the other hand to a *visceral* need to bite, to tear, to bark, it's *vis-ce-ral*, thinks O., but the thing becomes suddenly ungraspable, it shies away like a red shadow on the foreign shore of a dream of rage, and one is only able to speak of it in the language of doors and plates. Or by pushing someone all of a sudden down the stairs, these stairs or those, a living being, or through the window of some vehicle while holding onto the being by the scruff of its neck, one is capable of it

Sometimes, in the ramparts of my study up at the top of my tower image, I picture O. as part bull part dog, the bull is a dream bull, one knows this by its sluggishness and lumbering step, it lowers its head, which is large and bobbles and already fear is making me feel the curved and pointed shape of the horns, and in the cavity of its chest an old dog growls and weeps. O. is torn between the wish to charge, to gore,

12

to shred to bits, and an enormous regret. The bull ascends. Pauses on the landing. Raises its muzzle to the moon. Howls long wails full of childhood memories and fits of fury. What it wants to say I'd rather not know. The tone, arioso, the tone of the catastrophe arriving in the form of staccato sixteenth notes played in massive arpeggios. I will hit and be hit. Sometimes I see him as a thin black orphan surrounded by enemies, without god and without music. Always he enters the house without warning. I hear him before I see him. The cats flee

Every time we go to Montaigne O.'s phrase, "Cabirac, thirty-three inhabitants, one murder," comes back, at the bend in the little road that, with sisterly gentleness curls its arm around the neck of the Dordogne; as soon as O. glimpses the hamlet's delectable curves, something enigmatic cues this ritual statement. Enigmatic the repetition of this title, enigmatic the fact that O. introduces Cabirac at each representation as if it were the first time. If I questioned him, if I asked him: Is Cabirac the victim or the murder? Do thirty-three innocents or thirty-three guilty parties forever wear on their shoulders or in their heart of hearts the name of Cabirac? But I've never questioned him. Some mysterious thing has always restrained my voice. Each time, after Branne, when I feel rising within me the fever that makes me want to arrive at Montaigne as fast as possible and each time we close in on the bend in the road clothed in vines and cherry trees, I wonder if the encounter with the ghost will happen again or if the unknown soul-in-pain will have found rest. To heap enigma upon enigma, O. has never asked me if I wanted to know how the murder happened, what happened nor, if I didn't want to know, for what reasons, for this reason or not for that reason. There is a murder. There is murder. One can bury a murder under words one can bury a murder under silences. One cannot imagine a gentler sight than the small patch of countryside that frames the bend. Or maybe it's this vision of bliss that buries the murder. Or it's the days of ancient happiness that are buried – under the sign Cabirac. There can't be any murder in a place that is living breathing grace, one tells oneself. Which is when it happens – *BANG!*

Cabirac is of no interest to me. The only thing I love is Montaigne. One can't say that. If one says "The only thing I love is Montaigne" to somebody, one can kill that person without noticing. I've never told O. "I have no interest in Cabirac."

Now we leave Montaigne behind us and naveer toward the house. I think only of Montaigne, I am prepared for all sorts of concessions, prudence, patience, silences, detours, deserts, ruses, exiles, abdications, in order to reach the Tower. I've never said: "What's with this murder of yours?" It's at Cadillac that O. killed the cats, not at Cabirac. I am capable of closing my eyes for three months. One's jaw is never unclenched. One doesn't come up for air. One wakes up in the stretch of lane that takes us in a single leap to the Tower gate.

BANG! I bound from my dream. I was about to enter the little room downstairs where the Saint daily slays the Dragon. My friend P.A. had just told me that against the walls with their round arms leaned panels forty centimeters by thirty-five centimeters filled with texts in the writing of Montaigne, Shakespeare, Kafka, one after another as if holding hands, in the display's center one recognized the writing traced by my friend (the poet lost at sea), that was a surprise, I wasn't astonished, the Tower has always worked its magic on me, before the threshold cut to the exact size of the excited visitor, I quickly and silently thought that I myself would never have had the idea or talent to come up with such marvelous mixtures. I start to read, dizzy with emotion in the dimness with its constellated net of quivering – *BANG! "No!"* I shouted. O.

shouted: "It's not the last of your . . . !" I want to read another line, I want to go back to sleep, in the Tower. Both possibilities are barred. I am outraged. O. is in front of the door like a boulder. I can see that this is a construction, but *for the moment*, it has the consistence of reality.

A door that bangs, my Tower shudders. It feels like the first signs of our destruction.

*

When I write O. it's in order not to put B., which would be unfair and misleading. O. is one instance of B. Like you and me, B. is an army, one can't say it often enough. I note that Proust makes his narrator say that *in reality* he was not one man but *a whole army* and at that particular moment the narrator does say *I*, and in the army, he (that is, *I*) sees that there are some who are indifferent, some passionate, and some jealous, among whom none is jealous of the same woman nor with the same jealousy. Naturally one wonders if "I" takes the word *army* literally, and this is somewhat the case, it is an army, but not on the battlefield, it's a regiment on parade, a crowd rather, but orderly, rich in hue, and whose chests rise and fall with very different passions, and no doubt it's because we are an alphabet of beings that we write such varied letters according to the adversary or beloved to whom our soul devotes itself at this moment. Moreover each of our beings, or each of the letters that stands for us at this or that moment, is subject to universal change, that is the washing and scrubbing, make-up, quick costume changes, which take place in the dressing rooms of Time where the seamstress divinities, divinities inaudible and invisible, but even more powerful than the divinities of the telephone, do their work. In the army of B., O. is that moment which reacts mainly to those H. moments of *me* – what I am and what I wish to be, without fail, from the end of June to the month of September, allowing for compromises and parentheses during the other months of the year, as for a foreign body.

It's dusk.

I put mama to bed. I have fitted out her small boat for the night. The sleeper must be ritually accompanied by the objects essential to the crossing. Two glasses of different sizes, handkerchiefs, LittleBear brought back from London length twelve centimeters whom the sleeper tucks to sleep inside her pyjama jacket its two little arms outside. "He doesn't want to talk. But he wants to be rocked." What to do when one is old? Be rocked. He has fallen asleep. I've done all I could. She calls it my baby. LittleBear is her lastborn. When one is old it's better to have a little bear in one's bed. The great polar travelers, Shackleton, Gerlache, even Scott, each of them slipped off into the night keeping his little bear warm inside his quilted jacket. When one protects one is protected. Now we look at each other for a long time. Again. It's the departure. During the crossing each goes to a different country. I gaze at mama with all my eyes. I gaze at the shore, the landscape, always forever new changing, I gaze at the edges, the asperities, I put the finishing touches, now I gaze at her eyes, the new ones, that is, the ones that took shape last year. They have adjusted to the requirement of this crossing. One must see differently, further nearer wider more inwardly. The two eyes advance, not quite synchronized, one then the other, right to the edges of the lids, pause, they widen, produce a spark which grows brighter, glittering, undulating with a gleam of wetness, and seem ready to attempt their first flight. This is the adieu, I tell myself: we are going to be separated simultaneously one leaps with all the strength one can muster toward the face that one is about to leave. Always there's this struggle to hold on to the

16

face, the eyes that resist the forces dragging their face toward the separation. One is participating in the rehearsal of the last time, says my thought, while my gaze makes itself learn mama, shining bright and more than alive. "Shut up," I tell my thought. But neither my thought nor my gaze obeys my will. My thought laughs at my gooseflesh, my gaze trembles feebly. I see only the instant, it reminds me, I don't know how to keep. – I will forget you, my beloved, I see you beaming, I drink your light deeply, one day I will die of thirst and I won't find the sun. That's why I've been feeling so at home chez Proust lately, I feel I am on Swann's Way, one sees Odette's face for the last time before the first time, always one sees the Face for the last time, each time that mama turns her eyes toward me I see them veiled in a sparkling mist of adieu. I live in the land of Mourning. The dew stretches across the world, right to the places I believe the farthest away. I see all the moments of existence for the last time. I'm going to the Lighthouse I say. Yesterday with my daughter in the sky's beauty with the trees and the little walk and the absence of mama beside us, yesterday's stroll without her, I watched myself, from generation to generation, I also saw not with us my grandmother who is often my mother in my dreams and I saw my grandmother's mother looking at us with a strangely piercing and philosophical look, I was looking at myself, I was walking surrounded by absences with insistent eyes. I was in a state of adieu, telling myself: I was still on this side, on my mother Ève's side, today, I was telling myself in the imperfect. I am already I was, I was telling myself.

*

I am in a twilight state. This word twilight too acts as a poison upon my senses and on my mother's lips. We frighten each other. Everywhere – behind the doors, on the balconies –

there are disappearances. I shut the armoire door. My mother looks up, her face terrified, her eyes wide: – Where were you? – In the armoire. – I was scared because you didn't come back. I didn't come out of the armoire for a minute. Oh! What a terrible minute. A cat goes by. My mother catches it by the tail. The armoire might gulp her down too. She is staring past me. – What do you see? – The sky has fallen. The skyscrapers are drowning. The blackness swallows everything. I've never seen anything like it. It's all veiled. I don't know if it's raining. It's really very strange. The skyscrapers are almost gobbled up. They aren't there any more. It's crazy, it's crazy. Where are they? – In the armoire of the gods. They'll be back. – Do you think so? Do you think so? What day is today? – Tuesday. – So therefore it's twilight. What if we rang? Where is the young bell? She laughs. I am ringing for the skyscrapers to come out of the dark. – I am an old bell. She laughs. – I am an old lettuce head. Tossed greens. Did you buy the salad dressing? Can you believe it, those stone monuments? Swallowed up. And the old ladies, what do they do with them? And the cats? Do they come back? I'm going to sit and meditate. – What are you meditating on? – First the words next I ruminate the things of the past, I don't do much. I think time passes, everything passes. I have wristwatches. Otherwise you don't notice time that much. Strange to think people sleep half the time. Sleep, it's funny. You can write it differently. In big cities almost everyone sleeps in the armoire. When I get bored I rhyme I ruminate at night: I have to blow my nose before my eyes close. I'm managing but it's twilight. I can't read *Wind, Sand and Stars* because of the twilight. Poor Saint-Exupéry died young. The twilight makes me feel sad. All the books are engulfed in a thick black fog. Tell me a story.

"Suddenly, mountains of black clouds are flung onto the horizon," I tell that, I borrow this vision from the little book

18

that sits on her little shelf with its scratched mirrors, and that has such a tiny scrunched-up face, its cover torn, emaciated as a starveling, it makes you think of a dead leaf on the shore, or pretending to be dead, it's a small little tale, and it seems to me that it just happens to paint the black cloud that O.'s overheated mind spews out, that blows up the staircase like black scrolls of sacrificial smoke. There's a smell of burning. I forgot a pot on the stove, I hear vine shoots sizzle and the crackle of the skin of the lamb's shoulder, I see O. consume the oak, then the façade, I should have fixed the extinguisher I tell myself, everything here is mythological, but anything can happen in reality too. *Bang!* I hear O.'s voice swearing in the dining room. It's always the same swear word. By dint of use, the swear word becomes a signature made by a knife in a canvas the painter wants to punish.

*

August 2, 2010

Being holed up in hell, that is, plunged into a pot of boiling water like a crab without a shell, that is, without death as salvation since this torment passes, although in reality, in one's vision of the boiling pot torture, the pain is unbearable, the body, slumped in a chair in the study, has about as much energy to defend itself or flee as a flayed skin, and meanwhile the being, or the soul, of the condemned self sees itself suffer and suffer again, with no way out. The inferno sensation is caused by *being holed up in the interminable*. One hops from foot to foot, as if to evoke a change of place, this is not me this is the life in the body vainly trying to get away. One's imagination is handed over to the knife, any image that might envisage another construction is sheared at the eyelids. The cauldron bubbles with ghosts. All of them are there, the

19

youthful misfortunes that gnawed at my heart some years ago, that tore off bits of flesh, that knifed my hope in the back, and the older misfortunes that sit, stubborn, white, less agitated, on the benches of university amphitheaters, and who are not a whit less vigorous, just more patient and a little dozy, all of them crowd around, stick their noses in my face, my shoulders, and murmur, "we are ready to begin again."

Oh! The ghosts won't shut up. – If there's one thing I don't know how to do, I tell my son, it's stop the ghosts. – Monday your cat is going to die, and you know it, says a young ghost. – Shut up, I say. But the ghost doesn't listen, it's as if I was the ghost. – You can see, and you remember, this July 30th was exactly the same, and again everything is dying, you were pretending not to believe me, and in the end we are dead for good. Thereupon I see myself rushing back to Paris like a fool, cradling my cat, obeying the idea in flames that wants my cat to be dying, must die in Paris – die in my arms – today is Sunday and tomorrow is dying, I see myself, I tell my son, racing like a fool with mama in my arms, and at my back the thought that won't stop saying: "I'm ready to begin again," and me all the while running, acting as if I didn't believe it, I gasp for breath, I don't turn back. Everything explodes, behind me there's a conflagration all those ghosts waving their arms, and all my nearest and dearest I didn't save and who pushed me *onto the road of no return*, I see them I tell my son, my whole cemetery has burst and spread. To my son I say, voice coming in fits and starts in the effort to outrun death: "Everything is construction." But that too is a construction. How to escape constructions? I have hardly closed my eyes when a thick black fog blankets the city, buries the airport right to the tarmac where the plane in which my daughter is arriving should be landing, there is no more ground and I *see myself* seeing an ambulance arrive. I'm touching you, I say to my son, otherwise I would construct.

I'm scared and I haunt myself. Me and myself carry on a pointless dialogue. – Stop, I tell my thoughts, which of course plunge blithely on. – Dialoguing with yourself doesn't work, says my son. – It's just when I'm writing that someone gives me a hand, I say. But to write I have to be able to escape the feeling of speeding, death has to stop for a while, the senseless fear and the sensible fear must cease huffing and puffing at my back making calmness impossible, as well as the essential state of sleep in which the writing happens, without trembling, taking my time, I mean taking all the time that it needs for its journey.

– Each time that I find myself back in hell, I tell my son, I recognize this right away before any torture because the writing is stolen away: I am unable to defend myself. And immediately afterwards, at the very same moment, I lose mama. "Lose mama" means lose everything that is "mama," everything connected with "mama," that surrounds her, that is close to her, that represents her, that thinks about her.

Terrible dream (July 3, 2010). In Toulouse, after a day spent lecturing in a vast building, when it's time to leave I can't find mama, it's dusk. I elbow my way through the crowds: "Mama! Mama!" I call down the boulevards, I see the day end, I go to the departure desks, I ask them to make an announcement. The Public Address System mingles my high-pitched screams with its regular, booming sounds: Madame Cixous! Mama! Madame Cixous! Mama! Oh! Stay here and call until she returns! *Von dir will ich nicht gehen/Wenn dir dein Herze bricht!/ Wenn dein Herz wird erblassen/Im letzten Todes Stoss,/Alsdann will ich dich fassen/In meinem Arm und Schoss.* Chorale 23 tolls its knell in mama's German. This lady is not here! Call! Call! Is not in any café. We must find her! She's waiting for me, I know it, call call! Madame Cixous! She is deaf, please call louder! We are as loud as can be. Maybe she is waiting for you in another scene, in another city, in another dream? Mama!

21

Mama! Everywhere, the lights are being turned off. I call in vain. – It's time, says the Public Address System. I think all that remains to do is. – No, I cried, no!

And yet I found her, not in the dream, but where I'd left her in reality. Lying on her back in bed, where she waits for me to turn up and resuscitate her. She is shaking the bell with all her might.

– Mama mama mama! tinkles the bell. – I'm coming! I called and in vain, for however loudly I call, she doesn't hear.

I am sitting by her bed, I gaze at her with all my eyes, how beautiful you are, my old cat, you are old but you are beautiful, her eyes twinkle at me, five long white hairs glitter on her chin. – I dreamt I was in Toulouse, I say. – In Poulouse?! she exclaims. (I think *all* – *tout* – she thinks *louse* – *pou* – it's the same old story.) – In *Tou-louse*, I say. – Why on earth are you in Toulouse? she exclaims. – Lecturing. – What else? she says. She's not astonished any more. – In the evening, I look everywhere for you, I can't find you. – Of course you didn't, since I wasn't the one in Toulouse. – Where were you? – Wasn't I here? – I called "mama, mama!" – I didn't hear you, maybe I didn't have my ears in? – It was getting dark. – I didn't answer? Why? You didn't find me? But *where* was I? – In reality. – In reality. – And a good thing too, says my mother, reality itself. – And what's that yellow hat you've got on your head says my mother who hasn't taken her eyes off the beret during the whole of this tale. You'd think it'd been dipped in an egg yolk. – I'm looking for my chick, *ma poule*. – That hat (dipped in egg yolk) is full of holes, there's lots of air for the lice . . . I mean for the *poux*. This reassures her on the score of the poupulation. – What were you looking for in Too/louse? I *don't know Toulouse*, never been there. Pooh pooh, says my mother. I rang the bell, didn't you hear? – I was running toward you, I was calling: I'm coming, but in shadowland, alas, the voices are shadows of voices.

22

TURNSTILE

hoping without hope

At summer's turnstile, and for three weeks, every single morning I said "I'm going to commit suicide," or "you want to kill me"; at any given time of day one or the other of these statements would force itself upon me. The first welled up as I swayed over a row of geraniums still dark in the darkness five, sometimes four hours after midnight, naturally I didn't picture the means of committing suicide, I uttered this sentence the way one rips off a bandage, to squeeze out a pus of truth, in any case the risk of being suicided existed, I can say without embarrassment, a sulfur emanated from the house, and we all know that in such cases of exhalation anything can happen, a temptation lurks, an out-of-control pilot light, if the worst doesn't happen it's pure luck. By day, it was the other. This is a sentence which can't be uttered so easily, one must have dragged one's mind up summits whose pallid, cold look dashes one's élan, so that as a general rule one can't imagine reaching the trail blazed down the gully's other side except by swearing one is never going to make it. Should one make it,

23

one's head starts to spin and instead of proclaiming, with the desired aplomb, "you want to kill me" to the presumed killer, one hesitates hastily renounces bringing the sentence to its destination, in a flash one beats off all the furies on which one leaned, and allows oneself to slump toward the domestic ground, generally the kitchen, from which one exits, trying to stifle moans of defeat. For one is convinced it would be salutary, that there would be an effect of breathing after an interminable bout of pneumonia, to be able to shout this *Youwanttokillme*, one feels one's lungs hunger for a wrenching victory, a sensation one feels like a prehistoric trace in the pulmonary tissue, and by dint of feeling it gnaw at my cells and inflame my trachea it comes to me that this divided need, this howl of accusation one wants to spit out, this projectile of pain, is probably the ghostly offshoot of the cry of misery that one will have uttered with the force of a hero dying in the unlived instant in which one will have been exe-cu-ted, elec-tro-cu-ted, e-va-cu-at-ed from an undersea cave of security, excoriated according to Nature's law that condemns all living beings to be born by suppression, having paid on entry the ransom due to love's cruelty. All one can do is to forget the violence of those first loves intent on excriming, but in the end even the unfathomable pit of opaque forgetfulness seems to yield to the verypowerfulness of the heart. No burial I tell myself, titanic as it may be, that is utterly and for ever unshakeable. Giants wriggle under the pumice. Suddenly one remembers. Suddenly one forgets. What's fascinating is the rhythm. Very fast. Suddenly one remembers. The vision that erupts from the black blood's seething instantly drowns eyes and memory. One has just time to black out. One knows from experience that this period is boundless and timeless, its lava extinguishes it. The next moment one remembers, without space of memory, that existence was cut off and immediately reconnected, through a montage-collage of instants with

24

non-instants. The hyper-rapidity of the electric rhythm, more rapid than the power cut, means that one scoots right through death without getting caught. One escapes.

(Note: add here the note One. I noted. And note that you, as subject and captain of the Pen, keep a log. This is a journal of the Obstacles. All the difficulties, cliffs, reefs, long-sought long-unfindable passages that threaten shipwreck or stranding for technical reasons, problems arising in the narration when one finds oneself in waters where men have never before been, or, if they have, whence they have not returned to tell the tale – but technical reasons are naturally the sign or the result of mental resistances. Navigation is strongly and even violently perturbed. It is not unusual that one (One, I mean) be seized by the teeth of a giant gripped and gripping in the ice. For an undetermined length of time, but which always seems like an eternity. Add to these mishaps that the navigators of the extreme know all too well the horribly anguishing fact that the ice pack functions not just as force of retention, inhibition, annulment, etc., but also as a mirror. Then you get, in addition to the bodily torments, persecution through reflection, broken images, proliferating and fixed. One sees oneself in ice cages. This causes hallucinations: it's as if the mirror put you in the freezer and let you see the image that audiences of the future will take for "you." I note these anxious reflections on October 28, 2010. When the subject says, "I'm going to commit suicide" and then doesn't commit suicide, One says one, for one would be ashamed to say I. The shame is, however, unfounded, for one can perfectly well say and think in all sincerity "I'm going to commit suicide" at any given moment when this hypothesis appears to be either a solution or a frightening possibility.)

We are informed about these experiences by one of the almost supernatural optical phenomena that mystify the explorers of earth's arctic fields and the infernal fields underground: the subject perceives, far away, in the distance, an object in a vision that all the spatial and temporal data available affirm has just occurred and which is still occurring. One halts. Here are all the ages of time; all the floors of all the years of the staircase flatten out into a single step all palsied with age at my study window. How far away soon is, I tell myself, I've slept well and now I'm having a coffee I "take my time" having coffee, coffee time is as slow and regular as the motion of a pendulum, and I can *see* it pass on the face with twelve eyes.

A moment ago I said: "I'm going to commit suicide" and soon afterwards "you want to kill me," the tone is exalted, two voices articulate a theme two versions of the same clarity, the voices interrogate each other, revolve around a feeling of astonishment, a note of incredulity gave rhythm to each exclamation, not emphatic, but melodic, the transformation of horror into music through the effect of repetition. One repeats these sentences uttered under the pressure of real pain, one tries them out as one puts gloves on a passion, one believes in them, for to believe is to go before and come after oneself along the path of the unbelievable. No doubt about the quality of the truth, nor the musicality, of these sentences. They came to me on the very first day of our moorage, briskly, but with the explosive force of eruptions that science could have foreseen.

The first time I said it the way it came, a froth of fire at my lips. That sufficed, for the time being. But I realize these are scabs, flakes grown cold, drawn with broad brush strokes over a blistered canvas. I've seen paintings by masters of the emotions begin this way, spitting colors from the well behind the canvas onto the curtain's front. A cry from the heart. One finds this also in the syncopated interjections that stutter throughout the opening of the *Saint Matthew Passion*. Someone expectorates: "Who? How? What? Rrrah!" It explodes the vocal cords. *Wen? Was? Wie? Wo?* – I can tell you, it's exactly the same. Pain belches boiling syllables.

26

Wo! Was! Wen! Wie? – Herr! Bin ich's? Bin ich es! Oh! Sir! Is that me?! That! That which belches spits and grates do you believe that this what there?

It's that one doesn't know how to name – oh the caress of a name – this tornado that fells the skin of the heart with handfuls of burning needles. The fire spreads, one's hair catches, one has but one idea, turn in one's apron, besides it's already singed, there's a scorched smell, let's get out of here, let's drown ourselves, enough griping, enough stinking gutters, we are all swept along by evil and son, I tell myself – not that Evil is Son, I say to my Pen, no, not Evil and Son, no, see how the poison seeps into us, everything gets infected, my fingers seep ink, and under my fingers gallops the injured horse of my Pen, *O Evil, o Lamm,* one can hardly hear certain words, certain notes, one glides by an animal syllable, one is rushed past it: it's that the Passion is about to start. Bach couldn't hear the word *Lamm* without pity seizing him. *O Lamm, Gottes, unschuldig,* O guiltless lamb of God, Sacrificed on a trunk of wood, innocent, O Sacrifice for the sacrifice. O it cries famine. – No, I say to Pen, my terrified horselamb, it doesn't cry famine, it cries *family, Fa! mi! ly!* Do you hear, O Pen devoted to evil deeds, my Pen is my lamb, proof that no lamb is saved.

One cannot not be born, born to the knife and chopping block, we are born innocent, it's our fault, we are born for suicide, I tell myself, one can't not be born from Family, one can't not be a paw of Family, a slice of liver, a sliver of Family, one can't not be an asparagus stalk whose too long too weak body is braced by the rest of the bunch.

*

All I think about is writing, I was saying to myself, this I can neither deny nor be proud of: once mama's tucked in, I head for bed my mind on the writing that awaits me in the morning like my one and only love, whom I await once mama's gone to bed, and while I'm putting her to bed I think of her, I think about my mother, I think about the writing, I put my mother to bed I get the writing up I go to bed with her, I don't stop interrogating her, I call her – I note everything she says, I am perfectly aware that without her I couldn't live, I will never live without her, I protect her, I expect at any moment to lose her and yet she's the only being in the world who has never left me, even at the worst of times, I do nothing that doesn't come from her, that I don't share with her, I cook with her, I even manage to hold her hand during meals I give her my left hand, when I weaken in the course of the day, I loosen my grip but I continue to write "en italiennes," one dismounts but while going about one's business in one's study one thinks only of remounting, I am only interested in the animal, it lives within me as chronic as true love, that is, love the organ, a second heart, although at times it seems to me I feel her in my belly. I'm aware, to some degree, that this self-accompaniment is not to the taste of all my companions. The closest of my closest friends comes relatively speaking no closer than an exterior distance of great proximity. Things only turn acrimonious when someone wants to tear out my heart.

*

Seeking salvation I'd left Parislondon with this word "salvation" in my mouth like a host. Salvation, a word I'd never in my life used – which means that I'd never yet been in such dire straits. Up to then it was a solemn word, sacred, reserved, a word whose mystery I'd instinctively respected. A word I never thought I'd have to use. True, I did see people rush past in flames, brandishing this word, a shipwreck word, of poets in particular, horrified by families on the move. And now one

28

morning one finds it at the top of a page which might perhaps be the first page of our exodus, if perchance one managed to accomplish it. I stared the vocable in the face. Its shaggy, cross-eyed look, slashed with interruptions, regrets, repentances, illness, disorder, a dusting of phobias over its syllables, in short a grimace and one that crudely painted the states of my flayed-alive soul. There are words with astonishing physical powers, they blink suggestions from afar, I can't conceive of that, I only sense them sizzling. No getting around it, I felt repulsion, curiosity, submission, this tangled skein of contradictory affects stirred up upon contact with an unequivocal host, one of those relatives one has heard about, the crazy uncle. The one who hovers at the edge of the Family, the subject of an embarrassing legend, for he is a character, prone to exaggerate, maybe in error, maybe the opposite. Uncle Salvation is homeless, he gives nations a try, he's always auditioning this or that new world, once he was seen in America, once in South Africa in Johannesburg, Kafka's sifts through Madrid and returns via Australia, another story has him going from Bremen to Baltimore and back. One wouldn't like to be him, he is a chess champion, but when, on the occasion of a single stroll through the streets of Londonprague, he gives us his analysis of the modest and impressive odyssey that leaves him, what's more, utterly unchanged, forever elsewhere at risk, stopped in flight, persecuted by hope, changing his promised land as if it was his shirt, it didn't work out but almost last year when he planned to build a flagship supermarket on the island but the Congo awaits him, and while we walk along beside him as alongside the plague, we try not to give in to the cowardice advising us to disown him: we are his spitting image. Me too, I want to take to my heels, I want Peru, the country and the word, the figure, the grandiloquence of the traveler in Vain, the fluorescent shirt of the mythofme slayer of insignificances. Between us the differences don't amount to much finally. Each of us is equally ridiculous and admirable in his or her genre. Romantic poem? Satire? *Roman-à-clef*? Greek tragedy? Logbook? Life? Who knows whether in another autobiography one wouldn't be him?

Sometimes one gets carried away by this strange person who has written my memoirs. One has a Life. Hopes and tribulations included. One catches it through mental transfusion. A needle jabs, a sentence pounces and, in four words, Proust turns Senancour, this lasts long enough to make an Odyssey, and Senancour, as far as that goes, isn't too bad, but the transference is perhaps more titillating when one wakes up "old cow" Madame de Boigne for an ethnological soirée. Last week my son was George Green for a whole day whose fancied duration was forty-seven years. It wasn't the first time he'd become George Green overnight, this had happened before, I recall though he doesn't, in the exact same circumstances a year before. I note the coincidence. Each time we get together, the two of us alone, him with me with him, under a still-starry sky, the day after a shattering arrival in the house of reading which has been my small boat my safe shelter, for forty years, that is since the birth of this son, seated by my side on the tile margin of this volume of the memoirs, my son says: – Do you know the story of George Green? – No, I say. And, thus assured, the transmutation is instantaneous. I feel the adorable George Green's electromagnetic tremors at my side. Between us immense, thin, invisible sheet of glass, is this impalpable thing, which touches us, which we don't touch, which hasn't a human body and which nonetheless acts through mental and spiritual communication, this field, which we don't hear and which we raise in the nonexistent cup of his hands. "I pass my life," says my son. What a sentence! I say to myself. To be passing one's life! But the sentence hasn't stopped breathing. Like this: "I pass my life

30

– observing – cuts in the flow." Again "– the sentence – the life – passes – me – life – passed – observing – the wind – cut – cutting – the wings – of the windmill – busy – cutting – the wind – life – passing – my life –"

What a sentence! I tell myself, "fantastic," I say, "what do you think about this story?" my haunted son says, "you've already told me it," I say, now, everything is again, cut up, differently, and precisely on this very mound of earth, us, him and me, more and less, we are there, our lives passing, up to us to pass it according to electricity Nature's oldest law, like two beings, fortunately opposed by our signs, attracting one another, "tell it again," I say, "we aren't about to die" says my son cut off from Green, which means I am thinking that we are on the point of being on the point of not dying, that is we are passing our lives. Maybe that's Salvation? Sometimes, when the wind blows stronger, in proportion to the cuts in its flow, one has the feeling that Salvation descends on us in a gust of wind from Green's windmill, that it flings itself at us.

– Salvation is passing by, I say. – What a sentence! says my son. – All the same, I say, the Windmill stays. I'm keeping it, I say, Green's windmill, the divine miller. I think of Green, he's a gangly man, stooped, he never stops talking, like the extraordinary Nottingham windmill which has outlived his genius.

*

– And "me," each year *I hope to get closer to the Book-I-don't-write*, I tell my son, which is to say also George Green; and as a consequence I hope at the same time less and less and more and more, hope's material is modified by time, by the multiplication of the attempts, each new beginning loses strength on the one hand and on the other gains it in being and only being a new re-beginning, I see the same things each time differently and at the same time I assure myself that I will see them again in the same way, there is some work, forms emerge very slowly from the background of the scene, this is anguishing for time is not infinite, in another way it's reassuring for it's only after several years during which nothing seems to go anywhere, to move, that all of a sudden an image leaps forth, freed from the invisible ties that held it in a silent absence absolutely immobile, like a planet no astronomer or astrophysicist has since its creation even dreamt of and which swims into his ken out of apparent nothingness.

– And meanwhile, waiting for I don't know what revelation in I don't know what domain, I say to my son inhabited at that moment by the painful and jubilatory frenzy of George Green, I take hope as object of analysis, there's nothing more inconceivable, more perceptible and simultaneously more ungraspable, deceptive, decepromising than this state, most often lugubrious and rarely comforting, it is a torturer to whom one clings as to a raft, whose disjunctions disrepair the planks on which we lie they dislocate us backbone and soul.

When I hope, *I hope without hope*, you understand I say to my interpolated son, I trust in the dark, like a fool, I trust in the source, and it's this foolish madness, it's the craziness of this foolishness, the automatic springing up of this hope, which hopes even when I lack the strength to feel myself hope, that bears the wreck of me on its back year after year right to the point of embarkation.

And if there wasn't time, wind, twenty years of wind, thirty that I'll have spent staring at the wall of the closet in Montaigne's library, not seeing and by dint of not seeing, scraping away with my eyelashes at the vitreous blindness, until it turns up – as if painted by magic in a dream, in reality – the very image of my destiny painted, pending for centuries, over the mantelpiece? There is no Archimedes without sea, says my son, no Green without the wind on the

English hillside, no Montaigne without the rounded flanks of the Dordogne, Green's windmill is the spitting image of Montaigne's Tower. One sees right away that the Tower is a mill with invisible wings. The two bodies have exactly the same volumes and the same dimensions.

I had come to seek the great tale-less songs of the forests, the happiness without happiness and without misery, the a-human state. I aspired, I hoped, I expired the assistance of which the books spoke, and a few personal memories separate from me, whose usufruct had been withdrawn by the excouragement in which I was caught as in a pocket of amnesia, I had set the last of my strength to evoking bird songs by the light of the moon so varied it is said that one cannot not believe in some godliness, I still wanted to believe in the virtues of this recital, of which the authors I love state that when the songs of birds join with writing's crystalline voices, a musical phrase can, in our imagination, take the appearance of a nymph, a siren, and save our lives, that is, the threadbare fabric of the soul, the remnant of cloth, a wretched membrane stretched taut over the ravine of nothingness. When a book painted the instantaneous transformation of pale silvery waters unrolled between the light gold sand of the banks in scenes for eternity, even if the words lacked the power to warm me I still wanted to believe in them one last time, even if my sensation of belief was quasi-inanimate, distant, as if exterior to my heart. There's no choice. One must flee, one must *fi*, one must *nish*, one must anything in f, one would cling to a letter, to the frill, to the flounce of a folio of foolscap. What's more one doesn't flee, a flight goes by and sweeps you off, in whatever state we are in, a caravan of incoherent refugees, lit only by the premonitory vision of a ruin close at hand. Wrecks in a wreck, like the handful of former dignitaries whom Shakespeare tosses to the grotesque in *The Tempest*, Act I. The little, that we are.

But the result is that one jumps ship, one changes death at least. For, as one sees every time, one has this frog's instinct at the fatal moment, and suddenly one jumps, as if The Thing didn't want to, couldn't, die on the spot or die down dead or die from the first death that saunters by, one prefers the death at which one throws oneself or anyway one's body. Pride's last act. Or baseness's.

I'd left Paris to put a halt to the waste. We'd flung ourselves onto a bombed highway, the Family on the one hand, and me on the other, that is, the group me my mother, the cats and my memorious self, that sort of scroll or tall armoire that stands in for a character in an emergency. I am a first aid kit I tell myself, one of those constitutions of which tragedy gives so many examples. Generally it's men who compose this sort of crew equipped with the minimum for the worst and what one senses to be the essential baggage for any fatality. One always has a notebook, Kafka, Hamlet, Proust, and almost always a hat, a detail only apparently trivial. On this chapter I will have more to say, when the time comes. As kit, I have, for vital viaticum, three pairs of glasses each with different specifications, and three notebooks, 10 × 14 cm, the smallness of whose format proves we don't know what infinite means. The first notebook contains three years of my mother's life, my life, that is, in all its details. The second notebook contains the dormant gold of my dreams, their hundreds are my secret hoard, known only to myself – I naturally don't remember a single one – in my jacket I have a mine, an inexhaustible library of fables, phantoms, thousands of recordings of languages vanished from my brain but conserved in my pocket. And the third notebook is blank. The bare necessities. If I lost a notebook, first I'd lose my sight, next I'd lose my head. This can happen. To come back to the road, that it has been surmounted without catastrophe by our convoy whose

34

composition is comparable to the fleet, forever divided, of either one Ulysses or another – so that as one navigates one is constantly fretting about the other vehicle, impossible to control the hazards and the elements, one voyages in tandem, one sees double, one closes one's eyes to fend off the vision of a frightful accident to one's other half – this is because, as legend has it, the catastrophe naturally doesn't take place where one expects. It takes place upon arrival, in the hour that follows the moment when we saw ourselves safe and sound. It only takes place once we are safe.

*

As I sweep downriver, the expedition divided in two, my body is cut in two vertically from the sternum, I feel my head resting on my mother in the vehicle in which I have been holding her in my arms for hours, while my abdomen thinks constantly painfully of the cats incarcerated in an invisible automobile and delivered up to the gale, the way the belly of a mother, when she is without news of her children, especially of her daughters, thinks and begins to conjure up the image of the body beset by some awfulness of which one has no official proof. Lately I'd viewed my cats as my daughters and not as my mothers, hence the way I saw my mother as cat. This is the result of a mutation of my mother. That she should turn cat last year was decided in the month of October, according to me one can date the event from the perturbations around her birthday. Something to do with the turnstile, the train stop? I see her convulsed, I'm convinced she'll miss her hundredth birthday, she is drowning, I can't make literature trembling so, I am all for nothing, nothing to save her, a nothing of the end, suddenly, the tempest cut, as by Prospero, an exhaustion of life or an exhaustion of death, the hundred-year-old cart shoved under her feet, *she gets up cat*. No way to deny it.

Immediately set down with the cats, on the other side. She says: mehow, that's her German *h*, it is indeed her, and it is indeed them, those others, who answer meow.

My mother didn't use to like cats. Today love is everywhere, where once there was none. I wish I was a cat, my friend used to say. But this was hopeless, and perhaps it was a wish wished on condition that it be nothing but an artistic desire.

The Other Cold

I can, without embarrassment, say this: I really did spend the past fifteen months in the Antarctic, with the same overwhelming feeling of reality as if I had been there in a dream, the superior force of the dream having to do with the tenacity, the month-after-monthness of this sensation of dreaming in reality. During the first months especially, I had cardiac problems, vertigo, a sudden wobbliness in the legs that triggers the worst of my worst fears, and my eyes are still dazzled by the contemplation of the huge clotted milky slabs of bluish supernaturally opalescent milkinesses, I say milkinesses because milt isn't right, I have in mind blubbery thicknesses of a bruising-blue, as if one saw huge cubes of frozen milk spewed from the udders of vanished sea monsters, one thinks of the milk of leviathans, it's so fearsomely beautiful, the glacier chunks that heave themselves up in front of us glitter like optic witchcraft, sometimes a landscape ceases to writhe in spurts of pains whose steely blades of water fly over the boats, and subsides into a flabbergasted calm itself

37

as violent as the turmoil that this outbreak of calm has just stunned.

I crossed the line with some unknown persons who have become my Antarctic parents, I saw them every day, I knew them by a bodily trait, by precise kinds of behavior which distinguished them from one another, a look, a rhythm, linked gestures and intentions, for in these climates – if this word has any meaning in a world wholly governed by the unpredictable – it goes without saying that one doesn't talk to one another in depth but only in networks, on the surface, via telecommunications, the distances between us being multiplied to infinity, even at a distance of what would appear to be only three meters, by wind-blasted walls to which we add our own wall of garments, layers of fur, undergarments of paper, rags, we were a people improvised on the spur of the moment, whose past had never happened, all that remained were the signs of its absence: one preferred to not look back, and to constitute oneself a sort of compensatory past by assigning to a scrap of the future immediate the function of the future past. All this without speeches. One is neither us nor them, one is *one*. There is *who* too. And in the middle, mobile, drifting naturally, we keep, as if in a pot, a phial of warmth; not an artisanal fire, but a strong sensation of hearth, a sort of miniature inner sun, I pictured it as an animal spirit, that is a psychic animal, a ball of fur, a inhabitant, perhaps the most primitive form, the most archaic idea of "god," that is, the preservation of not-die; this feels like a presence in the midst of *one* of a very dependable, collective heart, never requested on the authority of a single *one* – the most elementary and most natural form, I told myself, of what on the developed continents one calls *humanity*, without knowing either how to write this word nor how to take its pulse. It's a dollop of warmth whose temperature is equal to that of the milk of human kindness – whose existence Shakespeare had deduced, as da Vinci before him, without their being able to develop their analysis of the mental phenomenon, one of those mysteries that slumber at the point of intersection between neurology and the psyche's traces in the immemorial archive of Life. *Life wants.* I had jotted this in the Magellan notebook: *Wish.* Or *Want.* Not "would like" even. A blank Wish like a diamond of ice but with the present of a subject that merges with this verb of being in a state of want. The extraordinarily harsh conditions of the Antarctic give this phenomenon a force which is beyond and sheltered from any scheming and any antipathy.

One knows nothing about one another, and no one knew anything about "me." Nobody showed any sign of having any information about my curriculum vitae, that I might have a story, that I might have published stories. Nothing is hidden or shown. One is tied by the winds and the icepack as if by threads of frozen blood. Most of the time I didn't even know their names.

But all this white this cold these jagged wastes, this gathering, had strung together over fifteen months a bottomless sensation of people, of familiarity numbing and yet extremely animated, similar to what we savor in dreams or when reading certain books whose webs have been secreted by the organs of individuals super-gifted with vital capabilities, untiring explorers, geniuses of curiosity, I think of the blessedness of Goethe or Montaigne, Kafka, Stendhal, of all those strangers whose charms bewitch us luckily so well that we forget that we've never met them for they have such a hospitable mental space that one feels recognized, expected, welcomed, and given a place, without more ado, without conditions, without contradictions, without commentary, without need for justification, without any remark, or contract, or pact, or issuance of a visa or sign of consent. An indescribable indication of kinship. Free entry exit stay nights transportation pains discoveries dizzying experiences of surpassing oneself, long moments of despair in ill-lit corridors, watery highways with fearful zoological vehicles, unbelievable scenes of torture such as exist only within the family and, on the other hand, scenes of voluptuousness at all hours, festivals of impertinence and downpours of eternity such as happen only at home with oneself, that stranger.

For fifteen months I was out of my mind except on Sundays – I should say thirteen months for in the final months I began to detach myself from the Antarctic family, I made myself a separate floe, I was tired and I had almost exhausted my supplies of inner amusement, of yielding to chance, of extreme passivity, my Pen was annoyed, it starts stalking my bed at four o'clock in the morning, mimicking still patient impatience, a warning, soon the harassment nothing can reason with, the little shrieks that plant themselves in my ears, in my cheeks, like the manifestation of a bird of prey's cruelty, but justified according to the right of each to act according to its nature. Besides this saved me, without my being aware of it: by January I had reached a degree of lethargy dreams can no longer breathe at the surface of. Silence, the ship is sinking. The dream book was adrift in apathy and no longer did I feel anguish at not feeling anguish any more.

*

"I spent fifteen months in the Straits of Magellan," I noted. I noted this on June 26 – months after my magellanies, I noted. I note that I haven't said "after my return," because there was none. Neither voyage out nor return. I note that I didn't keep a log, that I didn't intend to transform my magellanies into a book, that I hadn't given this any further thought since February 12, the date at which I began to hear the adored call of tower and windmill murmuring in the streets of deserted dreams, in the streets deserted by the dreams, in streets dreams no longer visited, all that remained of them was empty streets, erased memories of amnesias, painful traces of the erasure of traces that bleed you white. What's more I can't say that I really heard the call, in truth I began to feel that the call wasn't going to come, hence to be afraid, thinking only of the colors of days painted with the suns of the hills or of the Dordogne, or of Nottinghamshire, hanging around in front of these tender, complicated backgrounds, with their greens turning shades of rose, their silkinesses draped in waiting for the noble visitors who didn't come, who didn't come.

Only in June did I note and therefore recognize having sojourned in Antarctica. I was impelled by a sharp inner necessity, one of those astonishments that pick us up by the scruff of the neck, stand us in front of ourselves, give us a shake, enjoin us to pay attention to the fact that there are several of me saying *I*, that I do not understand my reasons, that when I open my front door I feel more violently foreign than when I spend months abroad, in books where I feel lodged as if the hotel had been written to satisfy my every wish, calm my fears, never ever contradict or disapprove my heart and my conscience. What brings us back to our reality, that is, to the terror, I noted, experience shows *is always some noise*. The sound of a very old voice, one thought snuffed out. For Proust it's the bell ringing inside him, the ring of *still*, a tinkling which becomes a tocsin. I wasn't thinking about it any more at all. Or maybe I thought no more about it. It could have happened that my life in Antarctica had sunk lock stock and barrel, like certain others of my vanished lives.

*

I was terribly cold – it'd be ridiculous to think one can paint the cold. Dante sings of it once, next comes the inexpressible

41

– without however ever thinking "I'm suffering too much, enough of this" – when one of my companions said we'll still be here in 2017, it set a limit to the unimaginable, I hung my soul on one of Du Bellay's laments, I drew some benefit from the suffering for I had hopes that in the end the unlikely would win out, I found beauty in the excess, at forty below I was changing the state of my soul, I was sinking below the level of literature, there were no more sentences, there below one moans, one screeks. Ulysses was accompanied by Athena. Du Bellay by his secretary laments. I could hear a barrage of my mother's piercing cries. This is new, or it's another language I told myself, she's cold too. Another cold. Besides, only I endured the cold as a kind of suffering. The other adventurers moved around so briskly that their undershirts were drenched and streaming. In truth *the Cold* I suffered is inner, I noted this in *my orange notebook* before the expedition, that is, I forgot it, I left it in the keeping of oblivion, in the notebook of forgetting.

We are animals who set down their last words. When the animal defender of life within us feels the ultimate cold coming, in which the other, the speaker within us, is careful not to believe, quick the animal deposits a stone, a word, an eggshell, a twig, a letter of a letter. One engraves. One scribbles. One digs holes. The end comes. – Quick! Mama! I cry. A letter! – Which one? – Come on, I prompt. – V. says my mother. Or is it "*Weh*"?

I'd forgotten the V. Or the *Weh*. It's the first letter or the death rattle which comes back, the sole sign on the white page. "V" 2005. Then nothing. Bleached shades of white, impassive pale pages. From the wan inexpressive look of it I see I was annoyed. Without this series of silences would I have forgotten the flight, the cause, the leap through the window, the strange happiness of being born far from the land of

Melancholy on the merciful banks of Magellany where nothing can tie up without having first lost its memory of the present? It's the only country (if it's a country) in the world where the entire candidate head and body is relieved of all his or her attachments, washed, bleached, and returned spick and span to one of those states of virginity viable only in the Norways.

*

"I'm cold," says my mother. Since, even under the parasol, it's very hot, I look around to see where this cold, which lays its painful palms on her shoulders, her back, her feet, can be coming from. I walk up and down the balcony. She panics. – Where were you? – Right here, across the table. – I was scared because you didn't come back. Why-why? Whywhywhywhy?

I can see what she looks like inside: she resembles a parrot in the grip of anxiety despite Felicity's presence. – Oh! A chill comes from far off to peck at the wrinkled claws. This makes the creature hop up and down as if shifting from foot to foot on a brazier of cold. It cheeps "whywhywhywhy" and then it chokes back "I-am-old! I-am-cold" replacing this with a look of apologetic astonishment. That's when, by chance, I open a book whose name I forget and whose author I don't know and whose first chapter I resist. Then an abandoned baby penguin enters, the baby sees its parents dive behind the balcony table and disappear, and as it starts to whimper and waddle up and down the shoreline in a flash I recognize mama.

It reassures me, to "recognize" mama's penguin cry, to cheep back, to envision the kilometers of rolling dark green, then the lacquered black waves one tries in vain to force open and let in the hope of a look, to understand in my heart's right half in what language and from what shores mama shrieks her desolation. One is about to be abandoned by one's parents, both say only a single inflexible farewell, at her age, mama's,

43

that is, a hundred years, that is, when one has had one's fourth birthday, but tremblingly, when one has four very old very powerless years behind one, and then these awkward little fins, and the too long dressing gown dragging its tail across the shingle, one cries why why with the help of the rusty pipe borrowed as throat from a parrot veteran. Literature embalms, I tell myself. "Mema!" cries mama.

*

Three Signs

Somewhere in these pages which cast at times a shadow of sadness behind them, set down in black on the icepack's white, the remaining signs of life. Urgent because a very strong drift affects the ice-field of this text, days last a few instants, unbelievable dawns breathe out grandiose and immediately funereal illuminations: for they are brutally snuffed out. One often feels, this evening: death. One's appreciation of distances is totally askew, one thinks there's a knoll, it's a mountain, and vice versa. At any moment one may lose what one has, eternal joy. Or at least one can lose the triumphal gleam of what one has.

Here's what happened:

(1) March 24, 2010 as I take down the navy blue folder that has always been devoted to my notes on "style," I notice on opening it that the cover's inner flap is concealed behind a glued-on sheet of paper. Right away I am struck by an empty memory. A tumulus one might say. I "know" without the least knowledge that my friend, the poet lost at sea in 1992, is there on the ground, covered up. Without my usual hesitation, I rip it off the way one rips off, unforgets, peels, ferrets out, seeking the pure treasure, proof of the existence of life before us, without us, the book of our dead and of our betrayals.

Behind the curtain of paper, a postcard: Giotto's *Lamentation of Christ.* The eight little angels flying in parachute formation have a balloon around them and in it the words *"we know all about resurrection,"* in my friend's handwriting. He signs: G., 1991. For a long while I contemplate the eight little aviator-explorers of the air, without once looking at the lower half of the picture where the chorus of mourners press. "We know all about resurrection" I would really like to know what those eight little apprentices know.

(2) The Dream. It calls itself *The Sign.* It comes to *repair* us. It is a very mobile creature whose face I don't see but whom I address, without hesitation, as a friend, for this can only be someone I call *Tu* – a familiar – and who makes me weep. All of a sudden I entrust or pour out everything. As always *Tu* is dead which doesn't prevent him being in fine fettle. The repairing begins with an acrobatic embrace, naked bodies floating, bound together in the top left half of the vision, it's blue and warm, the temperature of love I tell myself, for a long while we roll around, as in a dream, well beyond the time allotted for separation, without feeling the least resistance or fatigue. Then seated side by side on the milk-colored wall, whose cushiony stone is probably some kind of plant, *Tu* reveals "the sign which protects." Just before any voyage of separation, I learn, each puts his or her (right) hand on his or her chest (heart) and so contact is maintained. It's electric. It's simple and it works. I sense that we have here *the Absolute Sign.* And I tell myself that this last, long, fleshly, warm, tight embrace on the wing equals body for the years to come. I'll give it a try tomorrow morning with my father, I tell myself. I sense that this might *not* work: this proves that the guideline is absolutely concrete. On the one hand, this lowers my feeling of mystical exaltation to a more modest level. On the other hand, it reassures me. It is after all just a matter of technique.

(3) This same day I find mama "reading," which involves some intense peering, suggesting that the work has protuber-

ances or walls or scaffolding, all kinds of strange forms with slippery ridges her gaze clings to, she raises her eyes, one divines the slope of a cliff, she takes the measure of it, her face has the look of a bird during its apprenticeship, the irises bulge especially the right eye. But when I see the thing with my own eyes, it looks like a tiny old person, one of those thin booklets there used to be, a withered, crepuscular individual of limited readership, which seem straight out of a dream of Hoffmann's library, born of the wedding of noble ambitions with severely reduced means. In general these are poems dreaming of immortality. This thing, beneath its parchment, garishly tiger-striped brick-colored skin, looks like a cookbook, except it's too slim. My mother holds it to her face like a mirror. Leans in. As if she was scrutinizing her chin for hairs. It's not her face she sees now. It's a strange landscape looking back at her. – No, no, she says. – No? I say. She brings it up even closer. Her right eye leaves its orbit, swells. Mute, anxious: as if the eye wanted to get right up close and sniff – the object, the image. – It's ancient, no, no, says my mother. *Ancient* in her language is always *antipathetic.*– In what way? I ask. – The images. Don't interest me. No no. The eye enlarges, creeps. Doesn't let go. As if it was about to pounce. Slow retraction. – Images of what? I ask. Foreign to her own image. – Of a storm, says the mouth of my mother, keeping her eye fixed, immobile. But she isn't reading, I tell myself. She moves with loathing to the story's edge. – Ah! What a story! The storm is everywhere, I don't know why. It's an obsession. *L'histoire de la mer.* I glance at it. Impossible to know, whether it's the story of the *mère/mother*, or the *mer/sea* – or the one for the other. My mother stares in French at the poem painted in German. All of a sudden huge clouds in the sky, reports my mother, clouds which looked to be full of fear, but perhaps it's the sky that looks full of fear, they all lie down around the sleeping woman, says my mother. I

46

would like to close my eyes, but to read I have to keep them open. I think the sleeper must have been the mother, says my mother. She closes one eye, brings the other one up to the ridge of the image, where she halts on the shore of a great dark splotch that opens like a sex in waiting, there's a difficult moment here, roaring between the slabs of black ink like clots of stones, nothing is clear and one tells oneself that it is the sea. – *La mer?* – I ask. – *La mère*, says my mother, the ocean. As you can see, says my mother, they are wondering if *la mer* is still alive, says my mother, that's the question. – But who is doing the wondering? – The clouds. *La mer* is the one that's sleeping. My mother stares: the sea; the clouds. Nothing to be done. Now she's irritated, the mother, in the storm, she wakes, so to speak, she was asleep, she pulls a large hollow black tongue out of her sex like a big soup spoon. There, that's what the problem was! It was getting on her nerves, says my mother – slowly the eye steps back from the big spoon, retracts behind its lid – she is dancing, she is singing, my mother informs me. She was sleeping, but that woke her up, poor thing, those bad thoughts. You can feel it all. –Who wrote that? I ask. Wrote? The word, that's not it exactly. And my mother, who is unable to find any sound in her pipes, rummages, in the end she draws out a "ki" but so little, so pointy, not human at all, and more like the hysterical voice of that eye that saw it all. A gabble, the fluting of a distressed mouse. *Qui?* Who indeed? It seems to scare her. Now she is staring at this whole vision and she sees that it was none-theless a sort of book she was studying. She turns it over. It looks dead. There is no name on its face, either on the front or behind, there is only this baked mask, zebra-striped with black brush strokes that make no sense. Finally one finds: *Lenau!* That's who. A poet. No one I know much about. The name is calligraphed inside the storm, as if engulfed. I find this interesting. It's some poetry, announces my mother, the

47

storm. *Sturmesmythe*. "The Myth of the Storm." – It's a myth, my mother, docile, tells me. – What's a myth? I say. – Myth. It's a mystery story. Look at that! First the sea looks dead, but then she isn't. Or the mother. She starts uttering sounds again. At which point the cloud bends down and asks the question: are you still alive? Obviously she's not dead but all the same. In thunder it speaks.

– Don't you think it's an allegory? I ask.

– An allegory? The dead old mother, no no no no no. It's a mother. Or a sea. It's a *mère* or a *mer*. A mother. See, without speaking without moving, the mother sends her greetings to the beach. It's too sad.

It is not an allegory. My mother's nose is tearful, it swells up.

One looks into the mirror of a poem, the opening is so very small, one sees all the more deeply in, the storm is in the depths of the family, one discerns that: the family which is the storm – in the depths it engulfs, it tramples. The minute one looks. That's all the chasm wants: that one cast a glance, inadvertently, into the bottom of oneself. One knows it's there, but one believes one has come so far that all that remains of it is a memory, flat and yellow in a snapshot.

*

So, I tell myself, the family comes back, even in an old poem muttered by Lenau in a godforsaken groan, even when one ships off to America, disgusted by Europe and by the family, disgusted by the family one finds everywhere, by the Viennese, by the Swabians, by the French, then by the Americans, that is, by the family, pursued by the urgent need to flee the family which can't be fled, haunted by the unfleeable internal and external occupation army, even when one spends six hundred and forty-four hours in a stagecoach in

48

July–August fleeing the family, not a hope, one runs away from the family, one exfamilies oneself: the family comes roaring back, I'd made a note of that on June 29, upon arrival, I mean my botched departure.

Our family has been accompanied for a little over a year by the magnificent rumblings of true thunder, the choral side of things has been heightened, several times a week the sky grows black in the middle of the day, the weather tends to the melancholic, more exactly to an ensemble of different melan-cholies, so that if one melancholy seems about to run dry, it is overtaken and somberly revived in the next moment by the grimace of the following one, drowned in an excess of mel-ancholy, the corral side has also grown stronger I tell myself; meanwhile, hovering over our group of dumb animals, all of us of another species and each of us in a species not its own, the rest of the first chorale of the Passion according to Bach, a monumental hymn to oppression, plays on. "Do you hear that?" I say, in the dining room. Nobody in my pack of hounds hears this roaring polyphony and yet I am not dreaming: as if in a dream I hear the non-human crackles of disquiet, the banging of wooden limbs, those shards of breath, the ponder-ous, rushed, fearful interjections,
– *Sehet!* – *Was?* – *Seht!* – *Wohin?* If it's shrieking in German, I tell myself, that's mama's influence. On the one hand, I find my family turns up more and more often in the butcher-charcuterie scenes, minotaurs stamp around on the ground floor. On the other hand, never has the family's plant kingdom so flourished, there are flowers everywhere.

*

Observing "my mother": this becomes increasingly dif-ficult given the different kinds of disturbances and patterns, because she changes species often, several times a week, voices especially. The fact is she's inhabited or possessed by presences, human, animal beings, phantasmagoric visitations which, I suppose, she must in the old days have resisted, and to which she now leaves the door open, whether voluntarily or involuntarily: to be verified. At times there are long, scandalized speeches of protest, but chopped up, rhythmic, transformed into songs, at other times monologues that, flowing on and on, could, it seems, flow in perpetuity. The tenor of these recitatives is a sly mixture, knowing, innocent, confidences, witty observations, incantations that might be truly magic or airy inventions, half-digested refluxes of great historical events whose repeated resurgences and themes, for me surprising, make me think that, down in the basement, the lid of the maternal psyche, since the most ancient times the most hardened, is beginning to show signs of wear. All that has never been said, has never been allowed to come to the table, to consciousness, never occurred, never counted, never been the cause, never been named, never happened, never emitted the slightest perceptible sign of having been encountered, noticed, a quantity of famous people whom she has never in her life paid the least attention to, opinions she has never admitted having, and which furthermore appear in the form of detritus, or rather a fricassee of interjections, a comic dust of sounds of disapprobation, of expressions of pleasure in her disgust rise to her lips, and pour out in musical, lumpy streams. Bewitching exclamations beat time for these outpourings. It's not simply repetition: my mother adopts an ostinato and expands it, filling all the interstices with vibrations in *ha ha! he he! ho! ho!*, thus providing a rhythmic base for the voices. Indeed, listening, one is drawn more and more to the musical side. Perhaps one is approaching the most primitive layers of literature, I noted on January 15, 2010 while recording the following piece:

(One hears the percussion off to the side, something like: cha cha cha, but perhaps it's ca ca ca uttered without her dentures in.)

ME. – What did you just say?

HER. – ca ca ca ca ca
            ché
yoo yoo yoo yoo yoo

ME. – What did you just say?

HER. – ché

(now the voice does a riff on boo:)
boo boo boo boo

ME. – What's wrong, mama? is it yoo or is it boo?

HER. – it's boo boo boo boo boo
            ché
you think something's wrong? I'm yoo yoo yoo shless
the little old lady
the poor little old lady
I wasn't always this poor little old lady
no no no no
you know why? – Me neither
you know why? – That's how it is
I can't be young again
I'm yoo yoo yoo yooshless
and where is my cat?
It has ca ca ca ca oh oh eh eh
ca ca ca
has ca   that's what   yoo yoo
has cached itself
it's all up for me
it's not my fault
I don't know if my my if my my face
is up
it's not my fault
my cat is   ca   ca   ca
at my place? No. No no no no

51

It's all up

's ca ca ca ca

That reminds me of a friend who used to visit the asylum
do you remember it was A, A A A , it was A do you remember?
It was A 1933 do you remember?

Me. – I wasn't born.

Her. – Not my fault he went to the asylum

A woman showed him her backside

I am such a slut, she'd say

You remember that.

– I do remember, I say. It was Artur the rabbi who used
to go to the asylum to try to rabbi them, Miss Slut lay in wait
to ambush him with the song of her backside. Artur's problem was he didn't believe in the existence of God, he went to
the asylum without god, he was saying his goodbyes to my
mother who is off to England.

*

Every time I want "to compose a paragraph" on my mother's mutations, things escape me, the page rocks side to side,
the number changes, the place, a spirit of mockery seeps in,
de-rails, this even stops me sleeping, through perfectly efficacious subterfuges: I think I'm entering a room where sleep
and dreams await me, right away up she pops, this person who
announces that she has known me for a long time, with haus-
tility (an affect composed of authority and hostility, I know),
she hands me, over my shoulder, a meter-thick volume of
documents containing observations about my psyche, accu-
mulated over the years, to be summed up in a few pages, I set
to work, at my desk, determined to classify the material, that
is, to let the chapter take the bit in its teeth once and for all,
and poof! everything vanishes into thin air, I've only dreamt
that I was in the study of the dream, in reality I remain at the

door, deprived of sleep and light. I end up suspecting that if the subject escapes me this is because it is by definition ungraspable. I contraconduct myself in two opposite directions. On the one hand you will find me every morning seeing to the feeding of my mother, and to her maintenance in her present state. How I touch up the face, file down the dry patches of skin, I anoint a dozen dermatological beauty spots, one fills the cracks, one grates, one tweezes, one has the neutral and skillful gestures of a sculptor, the fingers know their material, I take care of the envelope of my mother the way I take care of our house, inside outside, I do the housework. This is natural. My mother's body must be kept up, my body, my house, the wallpapers, one begins up top, and one finishes with the feet. One has, with the toenails, the relationship at the furthest remove from the center of the family constituted by all the bodily members. The toes are like distant cousins; one admits without wasting too much time over this that they are a degenerate branch, misshapen individuals, ugly, small in size, arched over toes, broad and flat as little nun's coifs. At the family's other extremity, the hair looks down its nose. A success story, it has always been prosperous, athletes, curves, toned, at the age of a hundred it still goes blithely about its business. I ensure my mother's continuity, she herself lends a hand, she means well. – What does one do now? asks mama. – One lifts one's arms. – One slips on the blouse. So we travel in lockstep until the resemblance is complete

On the other hand and during this time, sometimes even in the middle of this soothing housekeeping, the house moves house. Everything is undermined. While up top, outside, one goes about one's maintenance work, somewhere in the darkened rooms a rout is underway. Underfoot we are mutated. I can't hold it against my mother, this din that penetrates the hold and threatens to dislocate the whole ship. One feels beyond the shadow of a doubt that here we have emissaries from those very distant regions which, while being at the borders of our own heads, appear to us foreign. "What's going on?" asks my mother. She is no better placed than I to know herself. At best she makes out the jig of the lice. This she knows. During the period of metamorphosis, this is a thing which fills her with horror, it is a clearing best skirted. "Don't go there," she says. Don't touch. The thing hides under tufts of grass, high and white, looking full of vigor where it stands thickset above the ridge, but underneath it's all crevasses and millenary wounds, don't even approach it, because right away you let out big snakes, louse-sized. Touch it, and especially put water on it and more especially that of a shower, and it goes wild: the big lice caper, and they make sure you know about it. They shout: poo poo poo, what am I saying, they holler, they bay like the lice my mother dreads more than anything. In the beginning I might have thought this a joke, a memory of one of those horribly amusing cruelties narrated in the goyesques of Wilhelm Busch. Never has one seen the slaughtered more hilariously sketched. Here, says the book, is the Hell where one splits one's sides laughing. What death pangs of hens accompanied by wild yelps of laughter. My mother has a weakness for nude humor. In torture she finds indices of wit. But that's not it, "no, no, no, cries mama, not the lice, don't cut the lice ice ice ice," and her terror is true. They dance, that's all. Me too now I'm scared of the Lice. I do what I can to avoid them. Since I don't see them, I have the trembling repulsion of the uninitiated. All I know about the Lice is that they are connected to infernal passages. When there are Lice, it is above all dantesque, it kidnaps mama and in her place it leaves a madwoman that she refuses with great outcry to be. I'm not going mad. I am not going mad. As always in these revolting states of revolt, the mad person's misfortune is to be attacked from within by the madman she is not. Obviously I know my mother is not mad, but I would be foolish not to at least take seriously the pain and the danger into which the madness throws her. For this, two possibilities: do one's best to avoid straying unwittingly or through lack of delicacy into the Lice Clearing. And since accidents are unavoidable, in case of attack: (1) never pour water on the blaze, for not only it doesn't extinguish the flames it fans them; and (2) of course stand by mama, shouting as loudly as she: Lice begone! In truth the lice never listen. One must keep one's head above the horror until what will have been the convoy of an epileptic assault is exhausted. When no nervous fuel remains, calm returns. No, one can't say this. Only for me does calm return. For my mother nothing has happened. My mother reads. Let me be more precise: my mother "reads." It's a kind of reading that takes the book to pay a visit to the ruins.

After a lice crisis I note:

It's a witches' sabbath. The Lice are masks, maybe they are masked Lice, maybe they are Lice lice, for my mother they are as lice as Gregor Samsa is insect. They've told her their name. If only I could see them! I'm a bit surprised this should be the sort of crowd that infests mama's cellar hole. If there is anyone I have always thought deloused, that person was my mother. The idea that she can harbor vermin, which breed on the waste matter of bad thoughts, never occurred to me. There must have been, either once, or across the decades, a tribe at the borders, or in the cellars or the gutters, or in the crypts or recesses of banks. Who's to know? With whom does one not live, I tell myself. With which whoms or with which whats next door or under the chair, behind the cupboard door, under the stairs one gets dis-infested. In the end the repulsed inhabitants have turned into mama's Lice.

It's late. Only on the eve of her hundredth birthday has the horde entered, or come out. It can vanish as suddenly as it turned up. The idea that an apparition is part of a series is merely a hypothesis. I could even, I tell myself, imagine soon experiencing a period during which I would regret the Lice. After the terror and the chagrin a kind of curiosity has come to me. Gratitude too. Thanks to mama's bouts of Lice I have been forced to recognize this evidence I keep so well guarded in the shadow of my thoughts: *I too must have a hidden horde. I am enhorded.*

THE FAMILY IS DESTROYING
ITSELF

"I wrote the next chapter ('We won't go again to the Tower') two weeks ago," – I noted on July 12, I examined it every which way, I built my tower, I divided it into rooms, I came out, I took it apart and put it back together inside out, I was always still nonetheless in this chapter, in its shadow, threatened by it, then I left "the completion" in suspense – in truth from beginning to end the problem was one of completions, of quarterings, of executing wills, of fratricides, I mean, of fratrimatricides, I have put off the finale although I've glimpsed or imagined I glimpsed the apocalypse, either in the first part or in the last, I've filed it away in a sleeve with its name on it and left it to chance, on the battlefield of my desk, and despite or because of its thickness, its weight or its battered beast inertia, it didn't slip down a crevasse. Whereupon I returned to the prologue and ever since then I keep getting further and further away from the target I'd nonetheless hit at the first try – as a matter of fact I could say the target hit me, the blow was so hard that having howled in anger and pain for five full days after the Explosion, I went on masticating angry pains, definitive, I tell myself, for the time being. *"Traumatism, tauromatism, mental tauromachies,"* I noted, they took my Tower and turned it into an arena, and the result, a total disaster for me, is that I keep seeing black, black zebra-striped with streaks of venomous carmine, my eyes stream furies I recognize for having read about them in Milton's *Samson Agonistes*: when one changes blindnesses, going from the blindness which sees everything in candor and milk teeth to the blindness which gorges itself on atrocious visions of crimes bred in the barnyard, pigsties and chicken coops of the unconscious, one is no more inclined to weep than a glue that paints the whole world *as it is*: this jungle of a City where jackels coo. To sum up, everything was already done or almost, "all that remains is to lay the book on the cadavers," I noted for I had a muscular and fearless vision of the chapter. "And yet. I've gathered my riches" – I insisted on noting, for even as I grumbled about being totally lacking in the essential (minutes, sheets of paper, space, plan, silence) and condemned to famine I glimpsed off to the side, in a corner of my consciousness, the little heap of papers I was stuffing into a drawer and which didn't not exist – and above all the dreams. Now, it must be noted, each page of writing and above all each dream becomes an obstacle, one more degree of separation. Instead of plunging toward the date of the contract with myself, I backslide. I scale walls till I lose sight of the main body of my building for I wall myself in outside of my object. I sink sideways deeper and deeper into the ice-pack. I contradict myself. Furthermore, I let myself get cold: hence I betray myself after having rebelled in rage against the onslaughts and betrayals of my circle. I forget my grievances. I no longer have companions who leap to my defense against the exactions of my entourage. My shadow's tired of me, of the inconsistency of my passions, of my lethargic vengeance.

I feel my fire dying down and I draw no lesson from this, I point it out to myself.

I wrote that, I note, a few days ago. It is July 27. Twice now I've noted the same delay with regard to my own deadline, in vain. Anxiety increases. I promise to drag myself to this chapter tomorrow at the latest. Hardly have I written *tomorrow at the latest* on a post-it, with the date of the promised tomorrow, than, tranquilized, I doze off again. Never say tomorrow, in the wee hours. It's like promising not to keep one's promise. Meanwhile (I note on July 27), little by little I've realized that this chapter really is the book's main building. Sometimes it's called "The Building." Sometimes "The Volcano." There's no shortage of landmines.

Unlike *The Castle* which belongs entirely and eternally to the invisible-to-K, and which exists absolutely and exclusively thanks to inexistence's powerful impotence, I tell myself, here one suffers from an excess of visibility, for the chapter as building shines implacably, one can neither forget it nor bear its constant glare without feeling woozy. This shows how much I fear fiction's hidden resources. It has been created.

*

This chapter is a powder keg. When it was made, forged, hooped, it was not in the least allegorical. It contained according to me as many seeds of violent death, bloody acts of vengeance, assassinations of enemies that is to say of persons close to me, sacks and pillages of neighboring mental properties, in brief as much garden-variety hate, if not more, as contained in the ravaged families of the Greek or Italian chronicles.

Initially one is like a wisp of straw that terror projects well above the terror, the fear and its feeble mortal representations, one is merely a groan in the supernatural bellowing, one twists and turns beyond the beyond of the beyond of the little-self, all the while expelling through the crater – for the top of one's head has blown off, and whatever one thinks spews from the gaping neck – appetites for destructions. That's how life is, that's how it is, you have no choice in the matter, homage to the carnage, this is the law of the family, destroy, destroy, either that or no family.

So this chapter, the book's Tower, I saw right away was packed with explosives. And this neither pleased nor displeased me. Everything that gushes out of the ordinary, out of the belted, like a rocket, all that lashes out and disfigures makes hay for literature, spices it up, concocts a sauce really intolerable for the tongue.

There's a body in the middle of the chapter room. There, I've said it. I say it. Immediately my Right Arm snatches it back. I stick to my guns: it suffices for me to say "there's a body in this chapter" for Arm to contradict me, bristle, he's about to deny. . .

For a good long while, this chapter ("We won't go again to the Tower") seethes from within, shudders and shakes and remains in all points similar to a little volcano whose jolts manage to unhinge the planet.

*

The family members would not hesitate to cut one another in two lengthwise, in their dreams, with whatever they could lay their hands on. They see themselves when they climb the staircase taking it by both ends like a field laid waste, and making it literally crack underfoot, for anger's effect is to multiply twenty-fold the mass of bodies convulsed with resentments. They rise up against each other in a sort of frenzy of desire, a negative desire, but a real desire, a delirium of attachment to the worst, an urgent need to feed on death, to devour each other that is to devour themselves since we are the members of our body. On the steps behind us gobs of flesh torn off by the teeth, by a jab of the fork, toes, little fingers. All this will grow back in traces of incurable rancor. Next, once the colon has voided its melted rocks, the volcano goes back to sleep, pillowed on excrement. The population of family cadavers who are rapidly transformed into immortal ghosts leave it indifferent. Moreover, I tell myself, some time after the butchery one no longer finds in one's notebooks the glories of those white golds smeared with incandescent bloods, or the dazzling vortex of the inner Vesuvius, or what was so exalting: to what point one was this tiny all-black stick figure with nearly invisible paws facing the majestic immensity of the eruption, tiny as the seeds of people drawn by Turner in a rosary of bacilli on the day earth gave birth to the gods through Vesuvius – to what point one was great, owing to being so infinitely small and nonetheless alive – the way one saw oneself when one painted one's self-portrait as Vesuvius while expostulating on the staircase of the house.

So, afterwards, the sound and the fury can seem to die down. The electricity is discharged, tension is released. Or someone is vanquished and in a clatter of antlers the loser retreats, head broken. In this case, however, once the vanquished gets her strength back one must expect hostilities to resume.

Or maybe the extraordinary Seduction exercised by truth-in-the-family, this fascination with the ways of evil, which we disavow, over which we draw curtains and white tablecloths, this taste for ogres and disgust, these bacchanals, these penchants for the stews of suffering, for the fricassees of severed paws, this ordinary repast of cold meats and cruelty, these scissor nicks in necks, in ears, these aperitif excitations dis-

61

sipate like the vapors of inebriation, this morning we diced one of the family ants – these are mainly the individuals who show signs of weakness all of a sudden whom one cuts to size – one was you might say inspired by an immemorial urge, it's a nervous tic, it's knee-jerk, one kills oneself a fly, not that one hasn't heard as if in sleep its voice's fearful buzz, but only in the moment after, the blow already on its way too bad, bang! –

– a body bites the dust, each does a few quick squats, three recoveries and it's business as usual.

*

During the week, in the Family, one saw nothing, and one doesn't want to. Just a dream, that obscene day, and no one remembers it. One buttons a coat on the Truth, and over the coat one slips a lie, woven in a film of false truth. The shouts and the shards, one drove them out like scapegoats. Each has returned to his or her own place, after the tempest, the mother is lying on her side on her couch with her cane. A sister notices that when the characters return to their places after the show, a brother finds his bed in the loo. No one wants to tell the Truth. No one *Wants*. One doesn't want to hear it. Is it still alive? Effortlessly one sets in the place of the mad Truth a better false one, a softer false true truth, all the truth wants is for everyone to allow it to say nothing, that way everything is false and no one is lying.

– There's a body in the middle of the dining room, says the Sister. – No, says the Brother.

– There's a body, I said. You can't say this, it's the thing you aren't supposed to say. This is the meaning of *Family*: there are never any dead bodies in the dining room. "Family" signifies: there is always a-body-which-is-out-of-the-question.

62

This body is really dead. If the body is a she, one says that she is sleeping. *La mer dort.*

It was me who said it. In the family, it's my role to say things. The body, dead. To say it. The word and the victim. There's a person in the family whose turn it is to say what mustn't be said. I'm the one. This year. This didn't come as a surprise. In the so bizarre way one expects something horribly inevitable to happen, and hence inevitably horrible, counter-thinking it, kicking it away, counter-expecting it day after day, notbelieving with all one's strength in the inevitable, acting as if one refuted any eventuality. One had no indulgence, no penchant, no fondness for this subject of anguish and worry. But in no case can one hold the subject captive in denial. One can't live, what's called "live," breathe, emit words, when one has a strangled body in one's throat. One must spit it out. We owe it the honors of existence. One killed it – no point in hiding it.

On the one hand we had a death in the family. One might compare this event to a reverse birth: O. and I engendered it, during a furious argument, and it was born on July 3. However, on the other side of the family stage, that is to say the Family, never had an entire firmament burned so brightly and so steadily in mama. A beam, I tell myself. And no brightness so unexpected, nor moon as silken in smiles as abounding in game in sly looks as the phenomenon of my mother, persisting, as unlikely as a broody hen on Cape Horn. I have an idea: the first hen must have been like this. Life broods over life.

Mama is better, I tell myself. The Clouds were thinking she was dead.

I began to say "there's a body" a few days after we arrived. Since this was an eight-day-old body, nobody *had* to

63

admit it. Such bodies are instances of the Invisibles, who nonetheless compose an important part of the Family, with which we on occasion find ourselves grouped. Mortality is rampant here, moreover our life in the secondhand Family is discontinuous, and rarely made much of. These bodies, who often succumb to totally unmentionable score-settlings, are recruited among our numerous shadows, all these members who accompany the titular members of the family that we are, our family tie representatives, these intermittent personages, genitives, whose roles we play, each time the family, for a few hours or a few days, makes us act the part of a cousin, an aunt, a brother of sisters or of brother, one of those agents of the cult of the blood, whose file is kept on record in the Family archives. A servant of the stifled plots of the Family by the Family. A functionary. As acolytes, our status is naturally more vulnerable than as ourselves.

"It is easy to deny the suffering and the agony of one of the intermediary figures among us," I said, just before dinner. I wanted to say it then, for during the meal I devote myself exclusively to my mother.

"I tell you there's a body," I told O. The subject O. has grown in size and volume, his presence on the landing, which is small in size, is bulkier, so that one can barely squeeze by. "This body," I said, *"we know who it is."* I said that to O. quickly and forcefully, in order to draw an undeniable, ineffaceable line, in the meantime. One dined. My mother said: "It's good! It's good!"

Is she aware of the body, I wondered. How to know? Things are known and sucked upon differently, down there on Cape Horn where my mother nests. Who knows, she may be capable of brooding a dead egg to life. Down there, everything is different, including hot and cold. Some days, my mother is cold from being hot and a minute later too hot which is a kind of cold, it changes all the time.

"My right arm is sore. Yesterday I had the biggest fight of my whole life with B."
I wrote that on dozens of supports, in dozens of attempts to report the scene, which resisted my efforts for the very reason that made me want to capture it at any price, because of the catastrophe's unbelievable savagery. It's as if the ant half-devoured by lava had no other aim than to paint in lava its own devouring. I wanted the *reality* of the catastrophe. But it severs our hands at the wrists. It annuls our eyes. It pounds our tongue. On the truest sheet of paper, the one closest to the fire, I poured out a vomit of sentences. No trace of writing there, it's wretched, such impoverishment, it's true that the last word of a human being is not a book, is not a poem, one is lucky if it's a cry, the call of a name, because it may be a quack, a flush of indignation, a whah! or nothing. What happened: *the other* dialogue, the one that had been underway *secretly*, for months according to the one, for dozens of years according to the other, in the course of almost daily exchanges, in the form of subterranean vociferations, by means of an entire system of transmissions buried between the bodies and the apartments, but "known," detected by leaks controlled or not, this interview, which could never have come to the surface according to one of them, which was bound to burst out according to the other, burst.

*

"You hate me! You Hate me!" says a sister.
One says these words with unmistakable passion: this idea of hate, with its name that has the magic power of a proper noun, is a tall figure, eyes on fire, cornea all red around the

65

irises where the gaze drowns in a wheelbarrow-load of slime and mud – this idea of hatred entered me with the passionate conviction of a love. With love's strength, one hates, one loses one's head, one hates, one is hated. And the breath, oh this sulfur of Hate, this slather of bitterness, this aloe one pastes over the letters of the word. "You hate me! You hate me!" one shouts in a frenzy of delight, and one really and truly feels that one hates with hate as if it were love. One is hateloved with hate, one is contaminated. And a brother says: "no." One wants to hate in hiding, flame without a torch.

"You hate me/You want me dead," one drums it out in a clear voice, one hears oneself say it a first time, then after the first trembling of the voice has been effaced, one repeats it, saying it twice adds force to the proclamation, but takes from its solemnity. In any case it's been said, I say to myself. It's been a long time since I said these words. They are so brief, so dull, a fistful of syllables, one doesn't have confidence that they can carry a message of such capital importance. These words should be called "Nabuchodonosor," for example, or "Behemoth." The other player can try to disqualify them. The words are like the body: one can kill it over and over. All one has to do is to act as if one didn't believe in death, as if within the family one was only waiting for a chance to kill it, and thus as if one refused the body the reality of a thought which would bend with regret over its entire history.

"What's going on?" my mother asks. She's raised her nose, sniffed. I felt chagrined: she doesn't hear. We are for her a silent film. I shouted: We are talking about *The Gold Rush*, it's not even a falsehood, I tell myself. Each word contains a little muck of reality.

This body, I tell myself, we know very well who it is. *It's us . . .*

But I am the only one who thinks this. This is how in the family there are half-dead bodies, half-alive. . .

*

O.'s Parabasis

This Envy adheres to my brain's deepest, darkest membrane this Envy is my darkness, O. says to himself, I have no choice but to Hatelove – *Haimer* – this is the dreadful layer of my brain, I can't make a single plan without having to drill through it, I think only thoughts wrapped in clouds of Envy, I can't go to the supermarket without Envy waiting for me there at the mental check-out. I repeat: I Envy her, I Envy Her, I Envy death, I have *en vie* of death, it's unlivable, always this black cloud forming in front of my desires, I repeat myself, the repetition is doubly painful, I bite my tail, I bite myself, my tooth aches my tail aches.

I remember that my foot hurts, now I remember my stomach is horribly flayed, at the time I felt a harrow roll over my abdomen, with its steel claws it raked my body right to the soles of my feet, I was lying on my back squarely between its four military wheels, the harrow flayed me, I was calling: "Father! Father!" everyone had abandoned me, you first of all, I was alone in a bulldozer's maw, my head yelped loud rending cries, in the claws of an SUV automobile executioner, the renowned Jeep, our so-called liberators turned on me, I was alone under the Jeep, O. tells himself, my whole life I won't forget, they skin me alive, the victim's blood pisses on to the pavement, is there a worse injustice than the torture of Marsyas? But nobody to deplore it, nobody to set down on a canvas the fabric torn into mauve and purple ribbons that bear witness to my fate, nobody did anything, who can say that the torture of a six-year-old child flung alive under the

67

wheels of a juggernaut was an accident, no one is innocent, O. told himself, is there worse injustice than the fate of the flayed? We are denied. Do people deny that the blind may bang into things? My skin is blind, and nobody understands that I have deaf and susceptible skin, at the least suspicion of a lack of sensitivity I pour myself out in blood-stained lava.

All "this" O. thinks in burning clouds, most of all at night in the storms of insomnia, but then one is battered by the whistling gusts, one groans in anguish without ever managing to turn the anguish into song. From the worldwide chaos in which one is engulfed, like the dreamers of dreams of drowning, feeling every detail of their agony without managing to escape from drowning, wake up panting half-dead clutching the dead dream, like a long-dead child, inert and faceless slipping away, one emerges crushed ruined empty of memory, flattened, the public squares are deserted; and of all that was probably a tragic civilization one keeps only the impression that one was invited to a ceremony and, only, like something gold, whose value one doesn't know, the word *Envie*.

– What's going on? my mother asks. She lifts her grief-stricken blind person's face toward mine.

– One has done as one *Wished*. One has violently stopped not doing what one wished. Wished to rip off the bandages, the clothing, the ties, the handcuffs. Wished to hurl at the others the darts and stones that one could no longer bear to feel worming and burning in one's lungs, wished to gulp down, to draw chunks of truth toward one's breast, one wanted to fire off prickly lines and one did. Not aiming at the heart but to frighten the beast, to make it back off, to prod it toward the exit, sling it as far away as possible from our self. I answered my mother in silent words. But in reality, disarticulating the words so that they would be easier for her to grasp, I said: "We are having a conversation about the economic

68

crisis." And by the time the words "crisis" and "economic" reached my mother, they had become the truth.

– Ten percent, said my Right Arm. Only ten percent of our commerce is in difficulty. The rest suits me just fine.

"The day after we arrived I had the worst fight of my whole life with someone I love," I noted a few days after my arrival, once the quake, which threw me for a loop, finally stopped making me shake all over. I still have the page as my witness under my eyes, with time it appears increasingly contrasted, background glaringly white, probably because the shards of the verbal outburst are thick and black, the letters misshapen, twisted, wrenched, no sentences, an exploded construction site, but strewn with fair-sized chunks of language, as if torn from a plump body

The page looks more like a painting than a story. In itself, at another moment, it might be an original work, I say to myself. "The remains of a dream of homicide in the family." I explain this thing of another genre to myself: the event that created this page belonged in fact not to literature but to performance. I see in this page, one of a kind, the image both poor and visually impressive of a psychic catastrophe. Sort of a pulverized hieroglyph. One pictures the body in shreds, a cruel puzzle, the pieces detailed live.

I see that I still wanted while it was still alive the
and I couldn't,
my right arm was dislocated,
this is a page whose brute strength
doesn't take the bit of writing

In the dream that I was dreaming of dreaming – for I was dreaming I was dreaming – everything seemed at first threatening, and the threat closely concerned me. To begin with I'd been put up, for the night that I had to spend abroad, all by myself in my mother's tiny apartment, upon which occasion I discovered just how cramped it was: so she now lived in two narrow dark rooms, one inside the other, it was so sad. You enter by the top, in this box there's a sort of dollhouse sitting room with allusions to armchairs cut out of blue fake leather and built in, pitiful relics of the old idea of an apartment. Under the seats, books moldering. I squeezed past the embrasure of this pinched pair of rooms by stretching out my leg till it touched the bedroom which was awful, below it had a bed at whose head was a window covered with metal shutters barred from the outside. I slept very badly, the Noise from the street rumbled around this wretched little shell: "I'm going to crack you, nut." Toward midnight I woke with a start. Outside – on the highway – I didn't even need to get up to see it – in a row, huge tormented trucks asleep in the cold which made them moan. Better at least to be inside I thought and to suffer in private. Then a frightened thought rattled me. The time! What time is it? I the punctual hadn't wakened! 11:30! Me whose long existence even as a cosmopolite has always been on time! I'm going to miss the prize-giving for the graduating class. I didn't know how to extract myself from this sticky misshapen little inn. Luckily in the depths of my misfortune mama is still alive I tell myself, not my mother of today in the cradle – no, the one from before, mama in the nick of time. And she reassures me: You'll make it – just skip the second act. I entered the third act on the run directly into the dark and still empty square, where, from the ceremony's stage, I slid discreetly and silently into the first place on the right of the dream. Darkness notwithstanding

I noticed that at each guest's seat was a gift, the same for everyone. Something old and soft and comforting emanated from this hidden and familiar object: a book, gift-wrapped. I opened.

At this moment everyone was wandering around the dream square as if they were just waking. The book was an eighteenth-century English novel. So such things still take place, even these prize-giving "days," which are so foreign to me, were twilit. Plus, I discover that I have the right to "a special mark of attention." They bring it to me without ceremony and without commentary. The package was shaped like a long sock made of brown wrapping paper, upon which my name had been handwritten. In black ink. Really though, I didn't check, it would have been rude. I asked neither: for me? nor: from whom? The sky was as grey as ever, quickly I unwrapped this long brown sack and it was as if I drew from the brown paper a scrap of Iris's scarf. A shawl, long, narrow, woven of silk in gently shining, lunar pastels whose origin I recognized right away. Those tones of old rose, fading into yellows dappled with mauves, this peel in the moiré hues of vegetables could only be a gift from Proust, himself. Proust who explained having chosen to offer me this, rather than to be here himself, etc., at the prize-giving. What a gift! I told myself. I was very happy. I couldn't have wished for anything better in answer to my deepest preoccupations, my most secret and frequent dreams at the time. I felt *marvelously* comforted by this piece of fabric. After all, since I have begun to dream of the book in which I am writing a delicate and finishing chapter of my life, I have always at hand – on my desk, in my suitcase, beside me, like the very idea of my work constantly taking shape, the supple and magic scroll of *the asparagus*. Later I will be able to say that I will in the end have written this book, which makes its dark way through dim, cloudy climates lit, feebly but firmly, by two candles:

71

my present mother, a gleam, a supernatural glimmering, and the asparagus, heroine, as we shall see, of one of the first volumes of this hoary expedition. To come back to the dream that I was dreaming I was dreaming, the appearance of the asparagus-colored shawl made up for all the pain and all the solitude. The rumbling trucks of the universe, that awful rusty old box that served as my mother's home, my uncertain and wobbly position in society, and I mustn't forget the war, the War which is the climate and atmosphere for the totality of the acts of my theater, all those evils and metaphors were attenuated if not eclipsed by a length of silk whose value is for me infinite, since it is cut from literature's fabric.

SAME SONG DIFFERENT PLAY

Let's take it from the top. Another song.
The voice is clear, quick
It hammers away ostinato: *Youhateme, youwantmedead*
If you could kill me you'd do it right here right now
It doesn't moan, it rings out *Tu é tu é tu é tu é*
– One can hear *tuer* or *tu es*: *kill* or *you are*
The other Voice, O.'s voice, thunderous: "I am what I am."
A cacaphony of dins: din above din below. The *Iwillkillyou* of
a hurricane, and the angry percussion of juggernauts roaring
deliriously down the highway, their *Iwillmakemushofyou*. The
Voices come from periods very distant from one another, so
that while they alternate they never form a duo they plunge
in turn into a different abyss. The staircase is traversed by
ancient or modern hallucinatory shapes. Rictuses from Greek
tragedy are printed over faces from horror films adding to the
dilated faces grimaces of cruelty. Suddenly, terrified, I saw
that other eyes had gained possession of O.'s eyes and were
edging them over their lids, out of their orbits. No longer

O.'s eyes, these eyes that bulged, swelling as if they wanted to cast themselves out of themselves, turn into jaws, devour, not see any more, devour, notsee, devour and gurgitate, push the puppet they couldn't bear to see into death's paunch, they were two frothing mastiffs, enraged with suffering, gnawed at from within by blind teeth, flinging themselves into action while secreting bloody salivas on the toxic object in order to be done with the torture of having the insect with its frightful stinging buzzing around. The Cyclops is now but the toothed crater of a single Eye gullet filled with a human carrot it wants to swallow whole, above all not to have to taste it, what it would like is for the hated body to pass like a stone down the esophagus, it wants to shorten, truncate, cut in two, swallow a section without having to endure the bad taste, reduce the odious mass as fast as possible, it would like not to *feel* anything any more, only kill, kill, stop time, the duration of the other, do the simplest thing in the world, cut life off at the neck, shut it up, that's all, turn it to stone, to have made it disappear and have it have disappeared, as simple as biting down on an ant – snap! – avoiding any contact with the formic taste that pearls in the cut. *Tu é Tu é kill kill* one's mouth is full of splinters of bone with a horrible taste, the Eye is as big as an arm now, how long there's no end, one is going to kill, two tonight tomorrow morning two more, every strophe one is drunker one grabs two at once and one cracks them open on the ground like two little dogs their brains dribble onto her sandals, one devours entrails meats haunches one grinds the bones one sucks the marrow, and this whole feast despite the desire to vomit what one stuffs oneself right to the bottom of the throat with, one has the horrified eyes of Saturn seeing himself toss back a pale pill of his own blood.

Several times in the course of the trance one thinks one can't jump out the kitchen window, one can't race across the garden, one can't run straight to the station, jump on the train for Paris, not only one has nothing, no papers no credit card, but the idea of exiting the family never to return is a vain temptation, without force, without hope, a tale for the family romance, for from here, on the staircase, no one escapes herself, one can neither grab mama and flee nor for a second envisage leaving the hundred-year-old toddler behind. In this play the characters are hostage to the sea – *la mer* – the clouds with their bellies full of wild beasts hover over the sleeper.

"Can she still hear?" they ask.

After an hour of this hymn poor in arguments, more like artillery salvos, it seemed to me that I'd already said these words, heard these outbursts, I'd just climbed two steps in the direction of my study, meanwhile O. was thrumming: "I'll take the train this evening, if there is one, if not tomorrow morning I'm out of here," the train was already in the body, vomiting and panting, "leave," said my Voice, "leave," what one comes out with during these rows – one doesn't think it, one doesn't know it, one has a single idea, fire the projectiles, who cares what happens, victory or defeat, one has but one thought: nourish the attack, reload the cannons. Grab the heaviest, shortest most hurtful words.

I'd already said these words. I sat down on the last step. I found it admirable on the one hand to have already said everything, that is, to have written everything, then right away afterwards to have been present during the rehearsal of this scene in the Great Theater where I play the part of author, and which exists, in reality, and not just in reality. This Great Theater also exists in the world of Dreams in which it takes up more space than any other building and any other institution. I find myself there in this or that state every couple of nights.

On the other hand, what I admired even more is to have forgotten beyond forgetting, forgotten right to the point of absolute non-existence, as a criminal forgets his crime as one forgets a dream, the Scene of the Most Violent Dispute, and hence having written it, having been once its author, having seen it interpreted in front of me, both outside me, and yet forever inside me, and to have nonetheless totally forgotten that I – I myself – had composed a scene to which I had given, as we do in the Great Theater during rehearsals, a title: "The Most Violent Dispute."

In May I was perched on a step of the Great Theater, I thought in July, I was reveling in watching a scene that the actors were not just acting but taking beyond acting to the place of truth itself, I was sitting on the top step of the stairs of my house, all of a sudden I saw myself back in May sitting near the highest tier of seats in the Great Theater – as sitting here in July at the top of the staircase. I was also feeling dizzy, I had just thrown myself head down to the top of the stairs to escape the Family disaster. The staircase had tremendous pull. It pressed itself into me like a hard law, ferocious, a proclamation, a clamor of reality. Whereas it is a hundred times smaller than the Theater. I saw it as it reveals itself only rarely in our history, in a flash unveiled for what it will always have secretly been: the passionate geometry of the setting of our lives' worst moments. Perhaps this has to do with its very theatrical structure, in fact, I tell myself: a white marble cage with black railing twelve meters high, a railing that resembles spears, like a thicket of warriors, like the bars of a jail.

When I had this house built, forty years ago, I wasn't thinking of theater, I was only thinking survival, escape, danger, it was all already theater but I wasn't aware of this, events crowded onto the staircase. I look at the staircase for the first time. The staircase has woken up, I thought. Or maybe we have overexcited it, and called up its volcanic destiny, or maybe the staircase has passed on its ancient messages of revolt into our boney frames.

I'd written a play for the Great Theater. Then I'd left the play behind. It lived on, on the other continent. In the scene called "Mayerling or the Most Violent Dispute" the Archduke cries: "You hate me You want me dead." Suddenly a voice mingles with the despairing voice. It's the Voice of his father, the Archduke's father. One hears him – him too – shout: "You want me dead." One doesn't see the Emperor. The scene is full of Voices. The actors, that is, the characters, on the one hand cry their mortal anguishes, with big melodious and terri-fied voices. The horror of being torn apart by the person one loves is in itself a death added to death. One doesn't see the father howl but his cries are reproduced, exactly, by the son. The Voice of the Archduke imitates the Voice of his father, it's very theatrical, this gives to the exclamations of the one the additional pain of the other. Hate is the great beneficiary of this massacre, it flits from one breast to another gorging itself on two bloods, same formula.

One hears the heart of the scene pound with redoubled force. One doesn't see the father but one sees his breath, his outbursts, the stage spins, the son acts both father and son, for the actor this is the role of roles, he feeds himself his lines, the bit, the death, he extricates himself, he chokes, he draws himself up, ever haughtier, and his head is a whirl now here now there, he is possessed, he possesses, he untangles himself from this powerful internal struggle his face smeared with the blood of Truth: you are one, you yourself tear yourself apart, what you accuse me of is what I accuse you of, word for word, ill for ill, we are the being in the mirror, the mirror is master, the mirror doesn't lie, like the Truth it reflects itself infinitely, you hate what I am, says the being, I am what you hate, the being concedes to the image, I hate you for being

77

in my image. Counterfeit! Yourself! You my son! You my father! They stutter and stammer. Awful to be cut from the same cloth! One can't kill oneself. One can only kill oneself. At times the Archduke gets carried away by his fury doesn't know if it is he who shouts "You want my death" or if it's his father, for in this battle of souls in pulling oneself together one can get mixed up, in a flash one puts oneself in the place of the other, which one must above all not do, and, as in the scene of the duel between Hamlet and Laertes, ineluctably one ends up exchanging swords, for there can be no error of which truth is not the cause, so there comes a moment when the Archduke, as he repeats with doubly calculated fury his father's killing phrase, recognizes his own words. Then his voice quavers a little. The effect of the crack is devastating for the spectator. One doesn't know who weeps for whom. One no longer knows who you are. One exchanges swords, one fights over the poisoned phrase. Thanks to this ventrilo-quism the Voice of the Father repeated by the Archduke is not reduced to mere reproduction. It is reshaped, reinvigor-ated, rejuvenated, more dangerous, painted the way he hears it, hyena-like, thirsty for vengeance, charged with centuries of resentments, it's the whole ass of the Empire up in arms against old age that is up in arms against youth braying with animal distress. Every time I watched the scene I was moved to tears. I always thought I saw an ass being martyrized by the masters of the human species. So the members of the family behave, I tell myself. They can't bear one another. They resemble and they execrate one another, all of a sudden they fall with their stumps of arms over the soul of the family, and often it's an ass which seems best suited to carry them off, an ass they beat. At the end of the scene, it was grey over the world, then greyer and greyer, the light dims the cold aug-ments, one has a heavy heart then one thinks one hears huge sobs, is one dreaming the being who suffers thus? Is one really

78

hearing the agony of an individual of our species? No, this is what happens when one distances oneself and is violently distanced from the house of tried and true feelings, those fashioned for family use. We have come to the mystery of the sadness in the pain, these great sobs that weep over themselves, it's the ass who is sobbing them, the innocent creature that suffers from suffering. And it doesn't stop. Terror has a terrible strength. The sobs pour out and are not exhausted. And then sentences like this: Why are you destroying me? Why do you knock me down in the dust and mud? they gave me goose-flesh. All the time I was thinking of the arioso and chorale 25 of the *Saint Matthew Passion*, where the tenor part evokes the failings of man, with, in the bass, the agony trembling and, alternating, on the woodwinds, the intervals of pain, I had goose-flesh, I was thinking: I could swear the tenor role is being sung by an ass, no human voice could make me weep like this, the voice of the soul wanders bewildered unassisted, among the orchestra's rigors what rises above these wanderings that don't listen to each other, that betray each other, is the song of solitude itself, of each for himself. Do I really hear that? I wondered. Did the theater's musician really take from an ass the mild and tragic accents which singers dream of achieving? The song of the ass reaches beyond itself, I am the ass, one knows not where.

*

I have always loved this scene, I tell myself. And I'd completely forgotten it. I'd let it live its violent life in the great hall of the Great Theater. A real scene, I'd thought, can never exist outside the Theater. Everyone's lips are sealed and no one is choking on anger. How long since we last saw someone in the family get angry to the point of wanting to run away, without taking the time to prepare her flight, for there's no other way to escape the approaching death of one of us?

In this scene one sees how quickly tragedy is upon us. Rapidity is the most frightening characteristic of a family tragedy.

During the scene the century's whole history was recalled, the loud cries of father and son mingled with past and promised wars, in the course of a few rejoinders nations rose up, others succumbed, revolutions of incalculable grandeur take place before our eyes, electricity is invented, one reaches the moment of hoping for the abolition of the death penalty

And suddenly a shot.

There was a palace, the palace disappeared, the dreamer dies before having written his dream.

The speed with which the present is decapitated.

The past tossed in the bin, it's not a head any more, it's a terrorized mask, empty.

Bang! A real shot? A real shot.

What could be more divine? There was a creature.

Bang! Decreated.

De-creation: a tenth of a second, and there's the end of the centuries of the Family, no more tales, nor notebook, nor diary, nor packet of letters, nor

A dog's voice

came to me when I was at the foot of the stairs. But I'm shouting, moaned the Voice, I recall Polyphemus, someone was yapping. One becomes substitute meat, I remember the young dog taste in the maw of the Eye, I was shouting at the top of my lungs:

"Peace! Peace! *In pieces*"

A life gnawed to its marrow! I held up my little finger. Here's what remains of the devoured body of my life, three little bones,

80

later I noted the war smell upstairs. One doesn't shout "Peace" peacefully, it's a sound whittled to a point in a still green olive branch one aims at the Eye of the war one wants to bore through the War mask's Eye.

All around us abyss, gulf, whistles of cyclones, now is the time to fling oneself from the family at the bottom of the staircase, shrieking "Peace! Peace!" One wants to die here and now! feast on ending, gorge oneself on Peace, put out the fire, the light, the adversary's head, anger, reason, all of it, in a single blow, the noise especially, the Noise, the desperate braying of the ass we are busy torturing. If one could die at will! I was thinking, I was beside myself, within me the fire raged.

"What's that smell?" my mother said.

*

A knife! O. was thinking, a crowbar!

Suddenly the phone rang, interrupting the scene. I told O.: "I'll be right back," I meant: I'll answer the phone and I'll come back and throw myself at the mouth of the dispute. I raced upstairs. The phone stopped ringing. I sat down on the top step. I'd said: "I'll be right back," I was all fired up, I wanted to prepare myself, but I'd lost the thread, and more importantly, the state of mind, in a few seconds one loses heat, the actor must make a tremendous effort to pick up the scene where he left off and find the same heat, the same bursts of thought, he must dive to the depths of himself as fast as possible, it's a test that requires nerve, humility, self-love, loyalty to the divinity for whom one is knocking oneself out, the Truth, who doesn't wait, who rushes back and forth between them, for Truth never favors one character, first this one calls her, then that and she goes to his aid, not that she's nomadic, but she is fair; that is, she always takes both sides, she goes here, she goes there, and when she's with one actor, that actor wants to wring all the force of persuasion he can out of her for he knows that soon she will be on the other side.

I could have not answered the phone. Had the telephone not interrupted the scene, who knows where we'd have ended up. In the scene of "The Most Violent Dispute," the Archduke constructs the future in his imagination. On the one hand, he fights to death with his father, that was yesterday. Now this yesterday begins for us. It is acted in its entirety by the Archduke. This also means that the past doesn't pass, it clings to the present, it doesn't let go, it plants its claws in our ankles, bitten, we drag it along, the wounds fester in the shoes, they open, no week without the wounds re-opening. So the fights are forever being dragged down by the increasingly numerous memories of earlier quarrels. On the other hand, before our very eyes the Archduke invents the new world. He sees it in all its freedom, he believes in it, we see him believe with a marvelous joy in all we don't believe in, we don't believe in friendship but he believes in it, we don't believe in the absence of calculation between even the closest of beings, we think, calculation steals in with his amicable atheist smile, we believe him our helper, the shrewd counselor of our two selves, for his friends he is as open as a mother, as a cove for a small boat, we don't believe in the absence of secretiveness, not even between the most loving spouses or between the most devoted lovers, but he believes, he believes in the fidelity in which we would like to be able to believe without nagging doubts and, in the tenderness which for him beams with such a mild light, we recognize that he is happy and that we are happy that someone be happy in our stead.

BANG!

What's that? Sweepers? Nimble servants, they collect a heap dropped on the boards, a heap of being, trailing long threads of bright red blood, one isn't done with being startled, one is done with being startled, there is nothing no one on the stage, one understands nothing, one must have missed a scene, did one blink, a moment ago one was dreaming, suddenly such silence, it is this silence that woke us from the dream, the great rustling silence that buries the dream under falling ice. One clings to the dream which vanishes like a dream, like a thief, off it flits, quick, quick, but this is almost impossible, then it is impossible – no almost – one doesn't let go, someone rips from our hands the lovely animated web of the Dream-of-the-blessed-world, and were there not this sensation of having let go of something making our palms tingle, nothing would remain to console and torment us with the nostalgia of the loss. If there is a sea which has opened and closed up again, it is lost to sight. The sweepers – one realizes that these are not sweepers but actors, hence their virtuoso speed – sweep up the mirror shards. A red thread. It's impressive. The shards toss brilliant, empty glances. One can think that this dead mirror is what, thanks to a technical trick, was maybe being held up from the stage earlier toward our secret dreams, with dumb joy we watched all our childish hopes come true.

In the next scene we are back in Magellany. Instead of the broken mirror a mangled ice pack. One can say this is true to reality at its most profound: there is an explosion. Life shatters. In the next scene another life is settling down at the antipodes. Which distresses no one, quite the contrary. Life goes on: elsewhere, in other latitudes, under other names. Or so I was thinking. On the one hand, this thought charmed me, on the other, I was in tears, I was sitting on the staircase, I was in the same prison, for the time being. The only change: the feeling of being incarcerated had intensified, I saw the prison house and staircase cage, closing around me, holding me like a corset.

How far away all the open spaces are, I was thinking. Here, I'm heading for the carapace. Yet yesterday, three months ago, I had a self who lived in part under the vast flexible roofs of a huge Theater, allowing the imagination to launch into projects without bounds. I remember the scene of "The Most Violent Dispute" with the chagrin that incredulity pours like acid on our heart. Everything was so big, happiness, hope, misfortune, once I was a tiger, thinks an ant, half-crushed.

*

The Archduke had Hell right behind his house, that is, his hunting lodge secretly turned into a library, but that evening in the house there is only Paradise, that which, on earth, stands for Paradise: an abundance of those books the only thing worth dying for, and which, for Mandelstam too, another dreamer who sheltered in a shack called Paradise, are written with stolen air. What's more there is only Nobody in the house, absolutely Nobody: except for the ideal self of the Archduke along with the three selves that most resembled him in the soul's mirror. In my imagination, I'd pictured these four incarnations of the Archduke's confident moments as four of the apprentice aviators who appeared to Giotto two thousand meters above the place where the scene of the Deposition plays in a loop. In the play, the scene happened very fast between the old earth and the new sky, the distance between Despair forever being reborn and Hope at its most infantile, most powerful, most poetic, is revolutionary. The Archduke is oppressed on the left by actual circumstances, on the right by the concentration and strength of the Vision. Between the walls of time, he draws a mental blueprint for the Future. He sees the image shimmer briefly on the ceiling of his study, he reproduces it as fast as possible, the way a painter does in his instant of illumination. Or a prophet. But he sees himself more as a painter, he is not melancholic, he breathes the air from on high right to the bottom of his lungs, moreover he sees tomorrow from above, he has a panoptic vision of it, he is happy that his self in a state of inspiration be multiplied by four, in a flick of the wrist the plans are so precisely sketched that the future gets ahead of itself, it leaps ahead of all the forecasts, it futures the present even before the latter has the time to call out to him, it is already there, like the friend who, hurrying to see to the needs of the friend, is already in the house before the friend has telephoned for help. In this scene the actors were so galvanized by the characters' dreams that they believed them, so that I saw real regret cloud their faces dripping with actor's sweat when the time came to separate. *(BANG! Exeunt.)*

Suddenly a shot rings out.

The Archduke killed. *BANG.* The telephone rings! But could it have been a shot?

"If you could kill me, you'd do it right now!" I thought. "Shut up," I told my thought, "you're fanning the blaze." Still, it was said. Thus the incendiary thoughts escape us. The fire singed the cats. They flung themselves at each other yowling their war cries, both had tripled in volume. I saw they didn't recognize each other. They saw death, such is death's power to change itself into us. When it happens, nothing in the world can stop it. We too have tripled in volume. Already I pictured the scene. Besides, O. confessed it, his eyes sought a weapon, and not for the first time I thought. His weapon of choice, I could see, was a crowbar

*

There was therefore, in the house where these exceptionally violent events were taking place, on a shelf or in one of my bags, the text of the play I'd written for the Great Theater, and thus without my being in the least aware of it the scenario of a scene whose theme and dialogues are practically the doubles of the violent dispute. It came to me that the play had entered my soul more deeply than I could have imagined. Other thoughts came to me. One doesn't realize to what degree one is subject to one's characters.

*

– So long as I live you won't write, O. gave me to understand, in his language, the language of doors slamming, smashed porcelain, cars giving up the ghost, cigar smoke fumigating the exhalations of laurels.

– I'm going to start writing again, I shouted, but what doubts and difficulties when *everything* is opposed to the flights of one's fancy, one has no air, no voice, and one's right arm hurts. Now O. openly led the charge against H. to keep her from writing, charge all the more violent as it was denied and turned against her. O. set off explosives on the staircase fireplace. Basalt vomit. Under O.'s thunderings one made out the accusations: you've always kept me from writing, you've invaded me, you vomit your lava flows into the veins of my life, you've devoured me, you spit me out again transformed into some other thing, you've knocked me down and crushed me under your wheels, flayed me alive from the diaphragm to the knees, stolen my skin, stolen my thoughts, sucked them into your beaks and replaced them with something else, you've injected my eyes with red images, you drown me every time I look at you, your looks are the cause of the breaks and deformations of my images, you weigh me down with an extra eye you petrify me, furthermore as everyone knows, you petrify people and don't know it, nobody ever told you because those close to you in particular are totally petrified of you, you have an eye that petrifies. H. crawled under the divan, she stayed flattened, plucked famished under the boarded-up sky for a week one doesn't write under the falling rock and rattle of lava, one cowers in prehistory. In the space of a second one is returned to torched scorched time, the gardens smoke, shadows are whipped by the spiny tails of brutes in the clutches of raucous terrors, shadows are crisscrossed by many-headed demons fired up by hostilities without discernment, rage is the blind sovereign of these monsters, I want to bite bite bite, the beast heads swivel and bite bite bite and bite themselves like something else. One cannot put out the fires that flare up in the cranial caves except by trampling and grinding the brains. Mush.

Now, the only way to free oneself, dissociate oneself, loosen the grip of these inner mortal attacks is to leap onto the ladder of the writing and scramble up it quick as a monkey, but really all you need is a paper stepping stone and a tree thirteen centimeters high *a construction* as foolproof as a rowboat for riding a riled-up ocean. Rise above it, rising above it is an easy, economical, efficacious way to escape the volcanic deliriums and as elegant as a mathematical solution.

But it is precisely from the calm even white light of mathematical wisdom that the house has been severed. The walls slime. The abrupt, deaf, hairy, frenetic law of the strongest roars from the entrails at the sticky bottom coil of the staircase to the heights of the balconies where the little bodies dangle and sway from the bars, strung up waiting for Time to devour them, grief-struck effigies of our cruel childhood memories. The deaths and the years notwithstanding, they remain unchanged, poor things. Suffering, wraths, resentments are as young as ever.

Me

I have been an author, I thought in deep dark secret, I was scrunched up into a ball over a step, my right arm hurt, my feet were shod in Chinese sandals as old as the world, their toes perforated by wear – dozens of notebooks, seven at least, in my pockets, who cares about the exact number since I didn't open them, I didn't write, I was ruminating on my pains, I am a stump of myself, I was thinking, I have for my model of misery Colonel Chabert's final "German grotesque," but I don't even know it,

out of *me* I was thinking – and I sensed with what feeling of affliction my voice emphasized the word *me*, "me," name of me, tortured me – out of *me* therefore, over there, armies arose, one can say this more or less, that I have brought some theater into the world, theater which is no less world than the world, and no fewer than a hundred kings and emperors, merchants of all kinds, captains of industry, priests, farmers, sailors, philosophers, geographers, lawyers, anarchists, workers, reporters, children, men, women, big and little old men and women, always of all kinds and all circumstances, rich ruined ruined rerich reruined, indifferent to all gold that is not the golden flesh of a word, honest, very dishonest and middling dishonest, foreigners from all parts and people who never ever think of themselves as foreigners, and, in conclusion, all of them kings and emperors, for everyone is, such is their right and it is the author's duty to create each human being in the image of kings and emperors. Me, I have populated, and I have crowned, I was thinking. Crowned and uncrowned, naturally, such is life, what matters is that the crown is there, hovering overhead. It is *me*, *I* who made them.

Who could believe this? I myself don't believe it deep down inside me. I myself don't believe me. When I don my crown of king and emperor, the mirror gives me back a fool's cap.

XOU, THE AUTHOR

– Lenau? says my mother, I think he's the one who departed for America. All the poets think they have to leave. Leave, people have no idea what that means, no no no no. Yes. In German one can't *partir*. Only in French. Another one who died young. Poor fellow. Poets die young. – Flaubert, I say, guess how old he was when he died? Flo-bear? I didn't know he was dead. – Fifty-nine, I say. He was a giant. – No! Really? Did that bother him? – What bothered him was the writing, I say. He lived bothered by it. – He drank a lot, maybe? – Not especially. My mother is downcast. Here they are all around us, the poets who die young, poor fellows, they prove my mother to be right. – Stendhal died at fifty-two, I say. – Stendhal, never knew him. Has he been dead for a while? And his father let him die of hunger, says my mother. – It's possible, I say. I sense that my mother's antennae are different from ours. – And Kafka? – He was born at the same time as Omi. – Did Kafka die young? – At forty-one. – Incredible! So soon! He didn't get on with his father. His father wasn't nice to him. All these men their fathers let die of hunger. And Balzac? Older maybe? my mother hopes. – Fifty-one, I say. – Impossible! He didn't have enough to eat! Him too. What's to be done? – Should I continue? I fret. – Joyce, says my mother, died at a ripe old age perhaps? Yet another hope shown to the door. He too died young? Baudelaire – here it's as expected: I think he died young. He's the one who went off into the desert. – Yeees, I say. – Not very encouraging, is it? says my mother.

"The greatness of Lenau, I say is that he thought of abbre-viating himself. That's what appeals to me in the case of Lenau, I tell my son, it's the idea of his having shortened the name, which was long, and even double- and triple-barreled, with several compartments, of cutting it off, and keeping only the tip of the tail, he could have kept the head, the *von* which is the neck, but he drops it, the crown, the trunk, the abdomen, imagine reducing yourself to the last syllable, that is to say, ten per cent not even of his property, but since *Nau* does not however suffice to make oneself understood on the telephone or in a conversation, he keeps two, the two last links of the chain. "I could sign my texts with my last syllable," I was thinking, not with the first but with the last, I caress this idea, I am in the dark I reach the point of thinking that Ci is an ant name and Xou is clearly the name of a tiger, and perhaps even a tiger name. I am rather proud of my invention.

Xou! Xou wakes me. You mustn't say "I wake." Xou whis-tled in the dark, the silky whistle of a bat's delicate flight. Xou! thinks a thought in the dark, and amnesia flits off. With a tremor of admiration I watch it flee on a wingtip as diaphanous as mist. In its place exactly memory palpitates . . . *le xouvenir.*

It all happened ten years ago "in reality," but given that it was an episode of metempsychosis, the indication is deceptive. I deposited this story and its life of Xou in a dateless oblivion. However the tale entitled *Xou* is collected in one of those books that you can go hunting for in library after library across Europe and even further abroad, for it shifts about, creating, wherever it alights, all manner of confusion. This tale has a prehistory. According to me, it was *invented* by the director of the Great Theater, an artist whose worldwide renown renders her to say the least indubitable. It was one of those days of ripping everything up and putting it back together again of which the Theater holds the key, a day when one rebuilds the world from A to Z so that it is not unusual to find oneself in the same nave with an Egyptian cemetery, the superimposed abdications of four kings under conditions such that there is an error with the crowns and one goes missing, causing one king the added anguish of having to abdicate his de-coronation, simultaneously one is trapped in the vast groin of a ship three-quarters wrecked and in the middle of these grandeurs laid low one feels a dizzying sensation of inner solitude, pettiness and mendacity. One is truly something obscure, one feels akin to a stool, and as one is rocking on three legs, Arne – the famous director and commander of worlds – who has in a glance taken in a "play" brought to her wrapped in haze – has one of her brilliant ideas. "The brilliant idea is that it's not the author who has 'written' this 'play,' but someone else, another author, a marvelously old and noble author, a dream of an author for a great director, none other, none other than Xhou Ci, in person, the first they say, that is, the most ancient of Chinese dramatists, his origin is moreover subject to doubt he might have been Japanese, this would surprise no one, in any case he is the predecessor." The word

Predecessor wins unanimous support. Every time they invoke him, they qualify him as the predecessor, they say Xhou Ci the Predecessor and everyone claps. The first to clap is the author (me).

I felt, I still bear the trace of the exaltation, the most ecstatic sense of salvation that I have ever experienced, an end to suffocation, the lungs' re-blossoming with life, emersion from the molasses of drowning, the newly hatched feeling of being torn from the half-death of nightmare, I was so saved that in retrospect I became aware of my, *by definition*, state of being incarcerated within myself, kept shut up like a slave animal destined to build a cathedral, then to carry it on his back, thereafter to be and feel responsible for all its defects and thus condemned to listen to the jeering, discontented, surprised, indifferent, scornful, sarcastic, disappointed comments uttered by the cathedral's visitors, for the not-discontented never peep a word, as we know since the days of Shakespeare. Never has the author, which I in secret was, felt lighter, a ghost of her live self, and as free as the dead. As for "the author," the "true," the Predecessor, Xhou Ci, no problem: thus far one has never seen visitors rise up against the venerable author of a cathedral. Free at last! At least as Ci Xhou who wasn't me and who for her part gained access to all the fortitude I'd never savored. I set cataclysms in motion, I built castles, I changed the course of rivers, I committed injustices, I killed characters every time the opportunity arose, only once did I think: the audience is going to think there are a lot of assassinations, but this was a thought of mine, an anachronistic timidity, which didn't last, and everything went very smoothly. I saw Truth. Reality as painted by the Predecessor had never been so vivacious, so faithfully cruel to herself, so intrepidly naked. I showed Truth, everything went very smoothly, the visitors didn't grumble, they were all satisfied by the Predecessor's frank brutality. At the bar they served a fricassee of infants. No one vomited. It was too good and it was True. Naturally the too good true can only happen once. Everyone was not in agreement except on this single point: Xhou Ci left, *could only* have left, a single play. The way Arne found one copy in a trunk, in I no longer know which Moscow, even I myself have forgotten, but the facts can be found set down in the forgetbook that went with the show. I was myself listed as the author of the adaptation and in truth I was. It is always the same tale of Truth. The emperor is too naked to be seen. In my tale Xhou Ci was Emperor and I was the worm.

*

I cannot be certain of being or of having been the author. It was a self so beyond my own self, so distant from me, so much more opulent, triumphant, Herculean, a richly brocaded thing that dances on battlefields, whole, in one piece, dressed, decorated, me, I'm just a bone under the stairs, my name is Hyacinth, I have never been a colonel emperor except in some pretense, chapters of novels, this I feel seared with truth as with a red hot iron. And yet, from a certain distance, every now and then, the other, that is to say the self spared by my burdens that is to say not crushed by the collapse of the cliff O. onto the ant, manages to get back up and I envy it, but naturally only in those moments when "the author" returns to me in memory, a very rare return. But right away, I don't envy her either. I can hardly be envious of myself, I tell myself. We have to believe that we are several and maybe a regiment, an army of *legitimate* pretenders to the crown, to the glasses, and to the pen. The author, that other person over there, perhaps recalls me as the me of the author, one way or the other it's all the same. The way I feel right now, if in this house things don't change I'm going to commit suicide, and

93

I'll be gone, for "a while" is not mentioned, "commit suicide" either, the imprecision doesn't lessen the truth of the devastation, when the tornado is in the house nobody ventures to reason with it nor to predict how the play will end. King Lear – right up to five minutes from the end everything can still be saved. *King Lear* has been my favorite play ever since I recognized it as destiny, I was twelve, I lost everything, while I was reading this story that nobody had ever told me about, suddenly it came true. I was Kent, I was convinced I could save the king, and as many others as necessary, it was a Thursday, that afternoon my father died, without warning *Bang!* before and without my being able to (understand, foresee, feel, and above all think), before I could have, I went mad, became old, Lear. For ten years I was an old fool ex-crowned and I still am. I lose my mind, my daughter, my honor, my son, my clothes, my papers, my grip on myself, and let's not speak of courage, all that can be lost, age, hope, aspect, sight, and above all dignity, several times a week, including practically every night, that is to say in the realms where I see myself in slippers shuffling across the tracks bent under the weight of a too big and too heavy coat, not seeing the train coming because of my perpetually weak sight, but I hear it.

I am amazed to see how it is so to speak impossible for me *naturally* to consider the life of the author as my life, everything that *made* the author I cannot *believe* that I can do those things, naturally I am careful not to admit this feeling of impotence to anyone whatsoever, to do so could cause us a great deal of harm.

The author-of-plays, if and when he is invited to speak in public, experiences during the entire encounter a feeling of strength and assurance, one enjoys it the way a flying trapeze artist enjoys the view. But let one make one's exit into the grandiose night and in a flash the feeling vanishes. A flying worm is all one is.

*

But for the dreamer of literature, what's intolerable about this activity, which is inactive, about this job that is not a job, about this waiting for something to come along that is dependent on visions as a sailboat on winds, is that one can't keep oneself going without the assurance of total solitude, whereas solitude is devastating, one lives on what is deathly, worse still, one lives on what deviates from life, one cannot speak wholeheartedly except to the dead, which I do, or to some of those among the living who are just as invisible and as unavailable as the dead, which I do.

Sometimes one goes mad, breaks into a gallop, tears off one's clothes, pushes back one's chair just when everyone is sitting down together at the table, one takes to the road, which is so empty one ought to be suspicious, a few meters on they set us down in front of an immaculately white, high wooden gate that should in itself be a warning, the person on duty opens it a crack, curiosity gets the better of us, and leads us beyond the few thoughts that might restrain us, might remind us that dinner is on the table, one enters and one is amazed to discover a veritable counter-city, a whole neighborhood of lovely white buildings, small in size, to our left are houses in the style of miniature Greek temples with colonnades, everything is closed up tight and seems to be asleep, it is elegant and calm (writing this I sense it is the land of the dead and I don't know it). One enters on tiptoe. And just inside are several little closed-up buildings with glass façades and texts I can't decipher, but that seem to originate with travel agencies. One watches the man who let us in out of the corner of one's eye for one is afraid that he might leave and bolt the high white gate, I take a few more steps, I would like to visit this sleeping neighborhood, then at a movement of the gatekeeper, I throw myself quite literally outside for I fear he will shut me in for good. Only then do I see that I was really alone and unconscious in the neighborhood of Silence Heights and that I found it terribly seductive. And if one doesn't leave dead, that's because, as with all who undergo these bouts of blank delirium, *one doesn't die of sorrow*. This one notes with horror or with relief. It troubles you, but it's also reassuring. One comes back. One is so astonished. One even forgets oneself to the point of writing to a niece, or a daughter: I am still alive. Naturally this means nothing. And this doesn't mean nothing. At times like these the writing takes possession of its words and its visions. It is nourished by such extreme states. The writing self thrives on pondering these inexpressibly calm and profound and attractive images. The minute the writing self exits its trance, it promptly robs itself, its satisfaction twofold: it is not dead, and it has nonetheless lighted upon something of value. In the example above, it's the blank whiteness of the architecture. This resembles a mathematical discovery: it seems simple and it advances knowledge of the human spirit. Flaubert and my mother wake up in the same manner. Flaubert: *last night I didn't die*. My mother: *last night I grew older*.

*

I want to spend all my final, last life, the unknown one, with my book, alone with my book, alone with my lover, alone with mama, these are solitudes that don't impinge on one another, don't interrupt one another, don't quarrel with one another, that glide over the sky's waters without colliding, whose pilots are peaceful and borne along by curiosity.

96

Each little aviator asks himself vast and fascinating questions, like a bee on a silver blue cloud, each bends over the sea's mirror wondering: who will I be in fifty years, what will I be thinking about, will you still be alive in me, *mer*, sea, what faces, life, will you turn toward me, against which wars, book, will you take arms, against what unimaginable cruelties will we be reading you?

I want to be alone, in my book, in my house, which is a book full of books, I was thinking, this what I want to tell O. above all, I want to declare my solitude to him, my malady, my book, my trip, I want absolutely to proclaim my silence to his noise, on all the doors of my house I wish to post a big sign: "Please don't come in (penetrate, shatter, break), Silence In Progress." On the front door I want to post: "Library. Do not set on fire! Do not smoke, burn, tear, allow counterfeiters to enter, leave supermarket 'books' strewn on the tables, on the sofas, in the toilets." I'm dreaming.

An acrid odor seeps under my window. O. is smoking, he has the right to.

Naturally one can't tell people: "I'm writing. Keep walking." At the neighbor who enters without knocking and says, "Just popped in, five minutes, that's all," one cannot shout "I'm going to shoot you, I'm going to jump out the window, I'm going to stick a steel pen in your heart," nor to one's family. Implacable are hospitality's laws, in the end the person who prefers to write is doomed to give her coat to the neighbor, to allow him deeper and deeper into the house, to console him for his mortal condition, to bestow a kiss on the plague, and, if the visitor is a family member, to wash his shirt and give up her life. I can't tell O.: "Don't be O."

My mother alone is compatible with the state of my health. Literature arouses in her neither positive nor negative interest, the irrepressible desire to enter without knocking, the sudden need to cause a hullabaloo, to demolish a sentence

97

with a phone call, she doesn't feel humiliated by my ardor for a paragraph nor offended by the joy or misery that a page causes me, she sees no difference in value between what happens to us in a book and what happens to us in the house: all suffering merits her attention, all creatures arouse her compassion. One evening, after I'd put her to bed, according to the rite, and as I prepared to jump on the plane and join the squadron, she rings, rings, rings. I think something bad has happened, I take the stairs two at a time in my nightgown, terrified, I find my mother in a state, sorrow painted on her face, at least she suffers for others, not for herself. "I am sad," says sad her sad Voice. "I think he's going to die." She shows me *The Love of Erika Ewald*. She is weeping. It's too sad. What to do? One was reading a book and the feeling of despair grew and grew, it would not slide past us but into us, one had tolerated certain sorrows because they were, if not attenuated, at least compensated for by the presence of beauty itself in the hotel, one was glad to have the vision of Erika Ewald without touching her, without speaking to her, yes, one existed in a state of half-mourning and this one had accepted, but she shone really, all one asks is to observe the shining, it's enough to light modestly but brightly the entire space in which we live, for my mother it was enough that the young man could go to bed after his long day's work telling himself that the sun would rise, Erika Ewald would rise, he would serve her breakfast, the thread was unbroken, one can bear great poverty, deprivations, limits, but on condition that there be *a thread*, life holds by a thread.

One can't get out of the house, one can't go on trips, I don't give a hoot about that thinks my mother, one can live one's pared-down days in perfect contentment, one goes from the table to the bed, from bed to window this is enough, this scintillates too, in place of forests one has planters filled with pansies and vases of pee pee pee pee onies, when one is a hundred plus rooms take on proportions others have no idea of, the house has its unexpected ups and downs, peaks, ravines, it's Switzerland added to Sweden-Norway, we also have the past and all its landscapes within us, one was, one went, too late now to cross the boulevard, one has Egypt and Chicago folded inside, what more could one ask, one is fed, one can get along without the REST, that unvisited country, but *it is essential* that there be *a thread*, that is essential, to draw it out, that we should draw it out, that, taut and fine, it tremble between the people to whom we are attached, that is, gleam between us, that it vibrate between the cats and between my mother and the cat, that everyone be held and hold, that no one be lost, left behind, cut off, that my mother be able to sleep in peace and wake up, roped to the rest of the climbers, assured that the whole world is there, everyone must respond to the call, all the creatures must respond to the call, one is a hen and one has all the creatures of all species for chicks, as well as the people who live in the books who therefore live in the house sleep in the pages and who are awake when one reads them. My mother weeps. I am not sure what to do. Exceptionally, I haven't read this book, I am face to face with an unknown danger. Groping, medically, I question her. The subject who is going to die, if he dies, if he is already dead, no matter who "he" is, how to help mama? I try. – Have you finished it? The book? – No, says my mother. It's too sad. My mother is in a prickly situation: she can't "finish" and see the character die who is going to die. But all the appalling hypotheses come to her, gather around her, and instead of a single death ten proposed their funereal services. But if she "keeps" the book she will necessarily end up coming face to face with death. So I say: "I'm taking it away. Try this one," I say:

It's less sad. Though all good books are fairly sad. Another Austrian, but not that sad. I laugh. I laugh at the Shipwrecks that crop up all over the house like weeds. I laugh at words with words. My mother says: "You laugh and all I do is cry and cry! It's too sad." It's all too sad I tell myself. I expect my mother to say: "Too too too." My mother doesn't say anything. Her little face like a tear-moist fist. I give her a hug. I take away *The Love of Erika Ewald*. He is going to die. I am going to read it. I've read it. The most beautiful thing about this book, I tell myself, is its reader. She stopped at "and the piercing moan of a useless brake."

– And Proust? says my mother. Proust too! I say. My mother is looking around her. All young. – It's the cre, says my mother. Suddenly a jaw, a shadow dweller, chomps on the word, and before she knows it, all that's left on the table is the word's head. Death ate the body. My mother, startled, looks around for what she meant to say. – It's the cre cre cre.

I wait. – Find it! I say. I have such confidence in her. I know she is searching with all her might, diligently, she calls cre! – cre – ! as if she were calling the dog, the cat.

– What's it like? I say. – It's sad. I think I think I know. It's when the su su the sun has not yet se se set, a little pus seeps out, and next comes skew-el skew-el isn't nice and the pus seeps out.

In mama's new country language swarms with parts of animals and hymenopteric words one grasps by a paw or antenna. When my mother manages to latch onto a segment of the insect, the rest will come. "Puscule!", shouts my mother, proud as punch.

If I've forgotten that I really used to be an author-of-plays, it's because I have fallen from the theater's heights. I am an angel bereft of her dreams. Aloft in the clouds, I woke myself with my cries from below, my earth cries. I was crying: "*I am going to kill myself or you are going to kill me*," and this was not in the play that I had written and in which I had no role, and therefore, since I was seated among the spectators, where I could leave, which I did when I grew too cold before the end of the rehearsal. Now I am in the play I didn't write, that I am not writing and in which I am forever being acted by other characters, I can't leave the play, I can't want to leave before the last act, I can't want the last act to be coming up.

Thus, when O. called, one Wednesday evening, at mama's bedtime (this was an evening when, for two weeks, a period considerably wider and deeper than usual, I hadn't been tormenting myself about whether or not I loved her, I'd totally omitted and forgotten to, I'd been off with the flowers and in those regions where man has so to speak never set foot), as I was standing with my mother on my left arm and the telephone in my right hand, the phone backfired so violently that I had no idea what I was doing. I laid mama down, I tucked her in, I saw the telephone swaying at the end of a cord, and it was, it seemed to me, myself I saw hanging in the next scene, I didn't know the play, I asked myself with a shiver: how's all this going to end, all I knew was that we were in the middle of several imminences, over here I braced to keep mama out the whirlwind, over there we were racing toward war. In my play (the one I'd been the author of) everyone shouted "*There won't be a war*," and even on July 31, 1914, people thought there she is, she is beyond us, she is in us, she is red and she has a monstrous jaw filled with teeth that are bigger than her own body, that is never shut, everything that happens has already been engulfed in the chasm which is in lieu of her stomach, meanwhile everyone was saying: "*There won't be a*

101

war," their mouths dribbling gallons of red water and helmet spikes fixed in their skulls and they say no no this is not war, they burbled soon we are going to wake up and all the beings already being swallowed up were howling like fanatics, as the jaws crunched them they swore it wasn't happening, lips gargling red froth.

"You shot!" I cried. I might has well have said nothing, the telephone's throat was slit, it was dead, and I had to put mama to bed without upsetting her.

In the eyes of my-mother-my-child, I am grown-up, I am beautiful, I am always smiling, I wear a knee-length sleeveless red dress, I wear high-heeled – but practical – sandals, my toenails are painted carmine, I am always there, I am: Mama.

O. shatters this image. He uses me as a mirror, he gazes at himself, he pulls faces, he thinks himself horrible, frightening, his eyes are bloodshot, his irises swim around fearfully, he breaks the mirror with big hammer blows, he bawls: "You don't see yourself! You don't hear yourself! You've never once heard the venom in your voice! The serpents that you take for hair drool into the cups of your guests. You poison them all. If you are around nobody else dares open their mouth. You are nearsighted as an eagle. You drill through brains from a distance. I'm going to kill you." O. grabs the lid of a pot and the big kitchen knife. I want to leap out of the red phantasm. But O. blocks the exit. He blocks the door like a rock. The only way out is slaughter. So I close my eyes, I act as if I hadn't seen anything and I hang up the phone as if nothing had happened. I am forced to recognize that in my "own" house I am outside, I am out of my house and out of control. Not that all the rooms and their details are not exactly where and how I left them before my expulsion, but that I myself am shut out, harassed, I can neither leave my house, which is my body and my memory, nor go on living and breathing here thinking about it. No state more nerve-wracking than that of being plunged into the unbearable. This space brims with sulfur. One word and everything blows up, and no one knows what the word is. Besides it's not just one word, it's now this one, now that one, over there. So one draws a dampened silence across one's mouth. And one moves through the streets of the house as if everyone was invisible, all day long all one does is avoid one another.

One July morning, I suddenly, urgently needed Truth, and for her to speak. Needed to shut the trap of Silence whose white thunder had been rumbling in my thoughts for decades; to split open the blankness of this Silence, whose monument of inert plaster stopped me scribbling straight ahead at top speed with all the spaces and times unrolling ahead of me, this Silence that I had to prudently circumnavigate on tiptoe, so that I was always writing off to one side, head down, ears pricked, and without ever being able to enjoy the panoramic view over the world's mystery. Now I wanted to shout at O.: "For fifty years you've dreamt of killing me *in reality*. If you could have killed me in a dream, it might have done the trick. But all your dreams are pinned under rocks, squashed. Now reality is all that's left. I take that back. Maybe all you want is for me not to be born. Yet another solution, but equally impossible. So you dream that I not exist, and in fact you inexist me, you don't in the least wish to kill me, but you consider, correctly, that you have the right to defend yourself and that this is the only way to close the oozing wound in your belly. You accuse me of driving on your surface, my four wheels equipped with steel spurs, and you deny accusing me. We are locked up in the Mirror which is the Family cage, we are in the cage occupied by the family actors, we are in the geometrical volume whose walls deform, one doesn't see that these are mirrors, the whole arrangement is programmed to produce distortions, each character is the distorted image of the scene's other character. Each character is convoked by his partner character so they can act the scene together. One can't all of a sudden refuse to play with the other person, this would be the same as suppressing the other's role, that is to say the other, you are an actor, this is your job and this is your mission. In the theater one character can leave and slam the door, it creates shock, the essence of theater. In the family there's no door, it's all walls."

But just as suddenly I had the conviction, the vision of the lack of *utility*, of the *Vanity* of the Verity. You can't live with the Truth. Dress her up in words and appearances, and she promptly turns false, hypocritical, simultaneously puffed up and emptied, she hates to be called upon, before you know it she collapses into ridicule and purulence. It's all false, I tell myself in dismay, it's nothing but a wormy construction, a tool for self-defense. We are misunderstanding beings. We are used for us against us in spite of us by misunderstanding. We are the mentally hard-of-hearing. In the guise of family and friends we secrete forms of characters into whom we insufflate formic acid. We *believe* what we say (and at the same time we don't believe a word of it), we believe only what we say (and yet we give no credit at all to the idea of believing). We are used and full of ruses. And by what? By whom? Who ruses us against each other, among whom ourselves?

I was saying to myself. And to this last question I thought it's Life itself, as it is in truth, not good, not fair, anxious, weak, avaricious, capable of every sort of trickery to keep on doing what one is doing, a killer each time one fears attack, hence a preventive killer. We are voyaging ants, who want at all cost to live and are ready at all times to give death as to receive it if necessary in order to stick to the fatality of our path. But what's the point, I tell myself, of telling O. that we are ants from the same anthill? If the ant O. believes he finds the ant F. on his trail, he will shoot first, parley later.

My Right Arm Hurts

"My Right Arm Hurts" is, as chapter, unlike any other chapter in any other of my books.

I lugged this brief and convulsive chapter, written toward the beginning of the month of July, around with me for weeks, wondering every day whether I was going to be able to tear it up, let it go, or decide to let it in, acknowledge it, not force it to confess, that is, neither disavow nor avow it but, out of respect for veracity, which is the tormented soul of fiction, leave it as is, scrawled across some big yellow post-its, tormented by hiccups, unfinished, like the victim of a shipwreck cast up on a meter or two of beach.

My right arm hurts. Surreptitiously O. has lodged there, between the two little bones of this elbow that I desperately need to write, I tell myself. It's always *someone* who hurts in our back or in our head.

Yesterday I had with O. (my right arm) the worst scene ever. The arguments collided off each other, the tone rose to the pitch of delirium. Who cares about the body count? The two enemy camps are joined by one imperative "thou shalt kill one another to the last man left standing," with the blessing of the Red Rage. I've forgotten the details. No time was wasted. Everything happened as in the theater. The enemies enter from the wings. A challenge is uttered, a challenge is accepted. The two actors fight to the bitter end in a crescendo everyone knows the result of, you might as well try to stop a landslide. A torrent of mud. One doesn't see what lies behind the mountain.

Why did the fatal quarrel take place this particular week in this particular year? Who knows: not for this reason, nor for that.

Several times in the course of this infamous week, I lose sight, thus: suddenly daylight is cut off, as if someone had turned out the lights – it is noon, I note, things grow dim, everything is veiled in grey, sometimes it's a black fog that falls without warning over the windows, the world behind this curtain is withdrawn, save in its ghostly form, in vain I light all the lamps, I remain sunk in despair: I see things completely differently, as if lost, everything up close but suppressed. Then the light slowly revives from its fainting spell but I am still unsteady and expropriated. This bizarre mourning lasts till evening. These troubles are not hallucinatory. I still clearly see the extinction of the bright stripes of the oilcloth, grown pale as cadavers. I have a problem with stripes and all things striped.

My right arms betrays me. My Right Arm hurts. Really hurts. On the other hand O. keeps me from writing. I spend a week beside myself, at the door, nerves on edge, unable to keep O. from keeping me from writing. The self I cling to as to the best of myself, the self I'm attached to, and that stands for me in the ranks of my peers, is no longer writing in my life.

Everything has for decades turned to misunderstanding between us, everything has always been misunderstanding and comfortable nonetheless

suddenly, late in life, we switch misunderstandings and it's war, the new misunderstanding is off its leash, it lurches around the rooms, smashes everything it can get its hands on in the kitchen, has a drunken haggardness. Not for this reason, not for that. One feels that life going forward can only be a series of border skirmishes. I'm in the dark, not for this not for that, one sees O. open the door. All it needs is for him to start talking in his O. voice and right away I'm on edge, I shout: "Give me my peace and quiet back. I want to go and write, I don't want people barging into my room, looking for stuff in my armoire, my whole room is in my head, I don't want anyone touching the shoulder of my thoughts, take your fingers off my arms, let me go." One ought not to begin to talk to O. Still just let O. cross in his own way the narrow threshold that divides our infinitesimal sacred territory from the vast stretch of the collective domain and blood gushes over the paper. O. knows that tacking the narrow strip of old-rose-tinted ribbon across the door-frame means "No Entry Before the End of the Afternoon." No, he doesn't know. If he did, why should he violate the ribbon? Violate! The word has a way of infuriating O.: "From this room at any moment a delirium of words swarms out, there's a flotilla of horseflies in this study," bellows O., the urge to strike at whatever moves, the cats for example, excites him; the cats look at him, apparently without taking sides but relying on their privileged status "I'm going to get a stick and beat them up," to each his pen. O. always has a stick on him.

I don't remember the details. One insignificant, silly sentence makes certain parts of my brain itch to the point of throwing a fit, I might claim that the unbearable first few words of a sentence were the cause of Flaubert's death. I don't even want to quote the words here. Toxic trivia.

"The family is destroying itself," I told my son. I said this on the phone. "I can't go there, mama," said my son.

We hung up. One of us cut the connection, maybe we cut it simultaneously. In truth, I hadn't said "the family is destroying itself." I was mulling over how to utter a sentence that I needed to phrase as a philosophical problem. I'd called my son who as P. is obviously one of the family characters, but only in his P. role; for as F. he also and even mainly exists as tenant-in-perpetuity of the Mills of Mathematical Life. I must have caught my son in a P. moment, and hence in a family moment, whereas I thought I was speaking to the Windmill. But right afterwards, F., of the George Green windmill, called me back. –What's the sentence? F. said – The family is destroying itself, I said. F. and I share a weakness for the mathematical animal objects. And we began to nibble.

I could hear my son chewing on the family sentence. – If I may say so, when you say "the family" this is a singular which is a plural. – Right, I say. (Crunch! goes my singular between the teeth of the plural.) – The singular destroys itself, ruminated my son, so the plural may survive. – But, I say (I could feel that I wanted F. to propose a marvelous mathematical hypothesis which would provide me with an escape hatch), on the one hand, for the species to survive, there need to be individuals capable of sacrificing themselves for its sake. – You are not capable of this, thought my son, and I read his thoughts. – But, I said, for the species to survive, the individual needs to survive. – It's tragic, we said. It's hopeless. –What to do?

My son said nothing. (Even I didn't know whether we were in the middle of it, in the swim of the Family, or whether we were perched on the edge of the water that the mill's grindstone was churning up, trying to think about sentence as text.) *Bang!* I heard the sentence crackle in the house. My son was saying something, over there, in the Windmill, but I didn't hear it. His voice was drowned out by a salvo of interjections and friable objects of volcanic origin spewing up from the cellar. A black fog fell over my study

   That's when I took the Decision. That is to say the Decision took me

Part II

WE'LL NOT GO

"We'll not go to Montaigne," hardly had the Decision been announced than I no longer knew what the exact words were that I had used to inform O. of it. My voice was loud and firm, of this I'm sure, but I perhaps said something more fatal. I was feeling the cutting edge of the end. I'd wanted to say: "We'll not go again to Montaigne," I think. But in reality I hadn't had the strength, or the time, or the imprudence, to lay down the law, "We'll not go again to Montaigne," this was a temptation, it would have weighed as heavily as "Mademoiselle Albertine has left," but I was caught up in complicated calculations of what the reality was, had I really not wished to go to Montaigne, I should have gone as if nothing had changed, discreetly, that is to say approach the thought of not going there lightly, un-insistently, above all without violence, so as not to provoke resistance. So I said "We must give up going to Montaigne," I believe, more or less. This is a more roundabout way of putting it.

The Decision having been taken in the neighborhood of

ten o'clock in the morning, I could have told O. the same day that is to say on July 5, 2010, that is to say on the eve of Monday, the day of the going to Montaigne, planned for weeks, and the only day possible in the year, since, for the trip to happen, there has to be a conjunction of the different compositions of time of all the characters involved to whatever degree in the outing. This combination of temporalities renders the outing as inflexible and imperative as a rocket's launch. Going to Montaigne is a construction as regulated, orderly, charged with memory and sense-to-come as an Easter celebration.

Now that it's all over, I wish I could recall the exact sentence. One would always like to be able to quote and repeat the three words that caused or accompanied or announced the onset of mourning, the end of a story or the beginning of a story, the first or the last, the sentence after which everything is forever changed, one would like to have the words, keep them, interrogate them, one feels that they hold the secret, they have thrown us off one path, pushed us onto a totally unknown path, they hold the keys to our destiny, they are as chiseled and finely wrought as magic keys always are, each tooth, each notch has its powers. I myself have lived in the realm of a few unforgettable sentences. I repeat them to myself under certain circumstances, when the shadows attain a thickness that leads me to the precipice's edge, on the brink I light them, they are the lighthouses, and though their gleam be too tenuous to grant me the splendor of a happiness, at least it suffices to keep me from the abyss.

I am almost sure to have thought: "We'll not go again to Montaigne" for this sentence is inscribed in several of my notebooks and, for numerous reasons both affective and literary, it would have imposed itself, not only for the times to come, but from forever. It is a sentence with a memory, it contains and recalls all the nostalgias and all the cruelties of many texts, and of several of my kidnapped and executed loves. None is more mournful and more loaded with sexual connotations. How this We is strong and sweet and rending and anguishing, like all the *we*'s, for no pronoun is more trembling and full of authority, more presumptuous and eroded by doubt than We. Who can say We without a shiver? The whole question of alliance, of community crowds in when one murmurs We. A dose of illegitimacy lets into We's crystal a slight bloody deposit. We? What an urge to possess, what furious innocence tints the heart of the subject who says *we*. And how desirous one is to say *we*, desirous and appalled. I adore and I mistrust this We. Will *We* survive? We is forever in danger of death. We needs to be able to count upon such consent!

Therefore I am not astonished, most of the time, to find We involved in a destitution scene. No sooner has We been assembled, promised, granted, than disjunction sets in. We is always already being undermined by its future dissolution. We is promised a tragic end. When I was at Montaigne with my beloved, we thought with fear and exaltation and hence of dying, we looked at each other, we looked at we, we were telling ourselves that in the *Essays*, at the heart of so many I's, there is the We of We's, the We of love and death, the heart, only, of an immense body with its marvelous, ripped-out heart, five years of We in a lifetime of fifty-four years, this is the proportion of we's in life, *We'll not go again* – Montaigne told himself and in order to preserve this We all by himself he began to write. And so, we told ourselves, writing came along to form a *we* with Montaigne in La Boétie's place. One takes part of one's own body, one draws it out as a shadow of the other on a piece of paper and one goes on we-ing. And nourishing us. I naturally thought this *we'll-not-go-again* both hypereconomical and euphonic – *nousnironsplus*, we'llnotgoagain – the sentence in itself is fascinating, it is so categorical, so assertive. It says no like a yes, a notgo is affirmed. It is a dictum that doesn't beat about the bush, an edict thrown out against the future so as to deny the future, *the invention of a denied future*. Which is exactly what we used to feel at Montaigne, when I was there with my beloved: one can't imagine a place with such an affirming volume, such obstinacy in storms, such steadfastness in deed, and into this solidity unique in the world was woven the thought of precariousness. And so, we said to ourselves, the Tower is the very soul of Montaigne. As our Tower we decided to build ourselves a small edifice in plain wood, like a double ladder. Of course, we thought, it won't last five hundred years, but, objectively, this light monument, a book in space, a notebook, a memorial, could, wood being less fragile than it is generally believed, endure for two centuries. I thought that this sentence bore on its shoulders, as Aeneas his father and me my mother, the sentence from which it descends, the unforgettable, that haunts every page of this book, whose cadence is inscribed in the least of the mental books of the world, those bathed in the French language, in any case. I thought there was a close connection between "We'll not go again to Montaigne," a sentence that I'll have uttered only once in my head, under particular circumstances, and "We'll to the woods no more, the laurels are cut down," a sentence that has been evoked, chanted, hummed thousands of millions of times, without my being able to account for the contents of the connection, though I feel it undeniable and deep. One says one thing, decisive, and right away one can feel it resonate with something else, whose vibrations of meaning ring out like the secret invocations that one is prompted to utter under one's breath in the labyrinthine cavity of a cathedral. It comes to me that I could have told O.

116

"We'll to the woods no more." Or maybe: "The laurels are cut down." Surely I said this in one dream or another. For fifty years this sentence has had a place in my personal, fantastic pharmacy, ever since the day I learned from Joyce that the inner monologue that runs without cease through his languages had come to him through the chance of an unexpected and literary inheritance. And the ancestor whom Joyce carried on his shoulders as Aeneas Anchises was Édouard Dujardin, the first of the textual laurel cutters, author of the book *The Laurels Are Cut Down*, a thing that had slipped out of Dujardin, and which he'd never dreamt could be the cause, the origin, the source of a literary revolution. In truth, it is Joyce, and not Dujardin, who'd discovered the magic of the flow, Dujardin having discovered the flow of the self's inner speech, called "stream of consciousness" or "courant de conscience" in French, but not the magical applications of the stream. Dujardin didn't extract all the possible effects from his own name, only part of the treasure, as is the case for so many miraculous inventions exactly contemporaneous. The inventor is not always exactly the finder. Joyce was indebted to Dujardin for the brainwave of electromagnetic fields in literature. Dujardin is a fictional character who existed in reality. He didn't know he'd had the luck to be shipwrecked on a new continent. And he had himself cut down the laurels, which Joyce had the honesty to bring to him. Not only had Dujardin discovered the New World of Literature without knowing it, but with the same insouciance, he had cut, gathered, budded the very flowers of the unconscious, without ever being conscious of having such a green thumb. I noted in my language notebook (where I note the flowers my mother invents) that Dujardin chose as title the second segment of the parataxis, whereas I chose the first strophe, the most clearly cutting. The cause is given *a posteriori*, without element of cause; one cannot all the same swear that it is *because* the laurels are cut down. What an unforgettable song, and one doesn't know why. There is a lag between what it says, which is terrible, and sad, and the melody's lilt. One rhapsodizes an execution. A cruelty is satisfied with itself. One doesn't know what one says, in the end. One believes one says something hard, mean. Whereupon one dances. One doesn't know what one is saying either when one names the laurels. There are so many different kinds, in literature as in nature. "We'll to the wood (or to the woods) no more, the laurels are cut down" tells you "don't enter," then right away after: "enter." It's enigmatic. And those laurels! What a bush, loaded with all sorts of connotations. If it's done, it's not worth the trouble of going to the wood, you understand? But go all the same? Hope for regeneration? And all these masculines that hide feminine sexes? Certainly when I told O.: "We'll not go to Montaigne tomorrow," I didn't tremble or shudder, I perhaps said "We must renounce Montaigne," I no longer recall exactly what the formula was, for the idea of not going any more or of not going to Montaigne was faster than the speed of my thought, the decision having been taken by the circumstances, everything happened over or above or beyond me – I remember that I felt a great calm, or rather that I ceased on the spot to feel. Happiness misfortune furor everything was broken off without any sensation of breaking, as in the strange and miraculous case of a person subjugated and wafted away from us by an anesthesia, wrested away without our being either present or absent. However, I see that in my orange notebook on July 5, 2010 I jotted: "torrents of anguish these past days. Decision: I'll not go to Montaigne, I announced this to O. True false arguments." I am now positive I didn't say: "We'll not go." In the state I was in, I couldn't, logically, say what I was thinking, I myself was afraid of it. I am sure of having felt impelled to say aloud and in a false voice (the true one was reduced to silence) "It is

118

necessary to renounce going to Montaigne." This was a pre-cautionary statement, a roundabout way of putting it, calculated, calculating, in which moreover I myself expressed nothing, it was the third person who spoke. *It will be necessary*, this is neither me nor us, it's the law. Plus it's a sentence that equivocates, the echo of a discussion slips into it. One says "it is necessary" (1) this is open to discussion; (2) any discussion is out of the question. Next up are the true false arguments. I'll say that one can't leave a centenarian mother all alone in a house become in her mind an orphanage, for hours which in her head become months, a real argument but which I will take as a fig leaf to cover the truth, I am really and truly afraid but this is not what makes the renunciation necessary, it is not this particular fear, it is this other fear that makes me renounce what no fear will ever have made me renounce, and then defers the blow of the decision, though in the orange notebook, the decision has been taken, as far as I am concerned. I see in the notebook I didn't write down O.'s response or reaction. I see, in the following entries, that in my depths swells and troughs are unleashed. O., in point of fact, was not shaken. Under the narcotic effect of the true false arguments, on the one hand, and on the other hand, I imagine, because it's not impossible O. may himself have thought: There's no way I'm going to Montaigne with this lunatic. I was mired in a swamp even before I went to the woods. The proof I couldn't have said what I thought is that at this date already I was no longer able to say We to O., but I couldn't yet tell him that I could no longer say "we," this would take place later. I may have told myself: "It is necessary to renounce going to Montaigne," and it was as if I had chopped off my head. This idea couldn't come to me or come from me. It struck me in the neck like the verdict pronounced by the hidden judge, the one who cuts the body in two after listening to the plaintiffs trade increasingly venomous blows

119

over weeks rendered increasingly rigid by frost. In the house the mental icepack was rapidly closing around us.

O. (let me slip this in here before it's too late) is the person with whom I've been on the most walks in my life, for with him, in the first place, I've been on all the walks that I planned to take with M. the lost poet my love, so as to have rehearsed (is this my playwright side coming out?) at least once and sometimes twice the walk my love and I would take, which needed to approach perfection, I told myself, in its details. During these rehearsals, I acted the part and occupied the place, on my right, hence in this case on the left, of the scene's main character, because knowing him like my heart I could better than anyone incarnate him, predict without fail the directions he'd be tempted to take, but also because I would not have liked O. to be M. So O. took my place in our peregrinations. What is especially moving when one has painstakingly rehearsed an action or event is to discover, on the *First Night*, to feel to what degree, with what unforeseen force, it is truly the *First*. Everything has been calibrated, everything has been fine-tuned, and the scene frees itself from our calculations and unfolds point by point on its own. One knows it by heart but it comes to us as if from the unknown. And secondly, I had taken all the walks with O. over and over again: O. likes to repeat his walks, he likes to walk past precise places and trees, before which he utters the same sentences every year, I'd always proved my friendship during these walks, always pretended I'd never before heard whatever remarks O. made with the delectable surprise of a first time. Overnight, when I decided (as per the orange note-book) not to go to Montaigne and probably not go again to Montaigne, it was nonetheless the whole walking part of my life I was giving up. I was perfectly aware of this. I didn't want to know anything about it.

Perhaps the time to go to the woods no more had come, but I don't recall having thought that. Decisions don't think. They gallop up, reeling and drunk, their manes floating and flapping in the pure air like breeze-whipped veils, they whirl around, make themselves dizzy and they drop like falcons on us ants, cutting us in two. Sliced, the ant-being lurches up, for one's soul is pegged to one's brain, and goes off wondering *afterwards* what caused the catastrophe.

Frankly, I said to myself, I could no longer make myself want to go with O., which was the one thing I couldn't say. I was scared O. would kill me en route and I wouldn't get back soon enough to look after mama. This would not of course be a simple face-to-face murder, no detours, like the famous mysterious Cabirac murder, this would be more elaborate, more creative, more innocent, that is, less interpretable. It would be an accident. O. would doze off at the wheel. He would therefore be absent from the event. I saw the scene. It was the inevitable accident that lies in wait for us, already in the house, needing only a road, a deserted one, to throw me out the window. Already at home we were ill, each of us displayed symptoms of his troubles. I could no longer use my right arm. O. suffered from vomiting and intestinal upsets. Going to Montaigne would only make things worse, probably propel them toward some fatal end. Never had the Tower seemed to me so lovely. I saw it as if I arrived in a dream, in a halo of sparkling silver light, you are the moon on earth, I thought fervently, you with your stars in your mouth and your laughing windows, you are my mother in all the brilliance of her prime, even better you grow younger, we age, you how-ever grow younger as you outlive us, everything about you is simple and profound like a scroll of the book of revelations, you are a cathedral refined to its simplest expression, you are godly, without a church, you are thinking, rustic and in season, I know you by your Grace, the same that resuscitates

121

my mother every morning at 9, she opens her eyes and she shoulders her life where she left it off, with a very powerful economy of means. You are worn and you are invincible. If there is a tower to which nothing ill could happen, or evil, or explosive, or male, she's it. The Castle burned, which is to be expected, but not the Tower.

Nothing is so charged with meaning. I have lost places, therefore I could lose them, and survive, though damaged, their loss. But if I had survived the unsurvivable, it was because I had the Tower. I lost everything, the Tower remained. In the Tower I have it all. I can't say how many sentences my love penciled in the Tower, on its skin with its dusting of plaster, in his elliptical and poignant style, they doze in the infinitesimal, almost invisible loops of these allusions of essays. I have lost dear friends, I have lost many selves I entrusted to friendships, and if one survives so many real deaths it's not just that one doesn't die of sorrow, it's that if one doesn't die of these mortal sorrows this is because, as the waves are about to engulf us, we throw our arms around the Tower and hold on tight. While I die the Tower watches over the last me and gives it back to me when, drained of strength, I start to sink. For thirty years (but perhaps longer, all my near and dear were still alive and none are alive today) I have not taken the path of a book without going first to the Tower as to the cradle of my beliefs. All my roads start from the Tower, especially the most fearful and rocky – the more obscure and humming with iron, rumbling with juggernauts, the better I feel the Tower's root in the distance resisting madness's attacks. Many times I have imagined everything that might take the Tower from me. I have conjured up all the inner and outer catastrophes, the water damage, the vandalism, the burning of whole regions, barbarisms as yet unknown and unconceived of, all the forms of destruction men could invent by following evil's illuminations – and all the deaths that suddenly decimate the people with whom one leads one's familiar life, in the strangely confident state of our days in which one takes one's meals without a thought of being scared of having one's appetite choked off by death, and all the deaths that, overnight, fill the telephone wires with tears, like Flaubert feeling himself succumb to the list of the deaths of all his acquaintances in good health even to the point of cutting off the breath of Bouvard and of Pécuchet, and losing Croisset's shelter. I trembled. But the Tower never swayed. She is as constant as a lighthouse. She has her eye on us. However, it does not suffice for her to exist in order to benefit from the effect of grace, for she is. It is also necessary *to go there*.

Going to the Tower is an act of a quasi-religious profundity and the religion is Friendship. It is inconceivable and furthermore useless to go to Montaigne otherwise than worshipfully, lightly, excitedly. And giving thanks to Literature. No friendship without Literature, this noble commerce, Montaigne thought. Always this long and tender conversation, the friendship of which I speak and the friendship of which I speak to myself; I speak to myself and it's to you and thanks to you that I speak, that I speak to myself of you by and through Literature, that is, by correspondence. I write you. I take the road of friendship and literature in order to paint you. Going to Montaigne is a Grand Tour of love and of meditation on the paper of reality. One goes there in friendship, thinking along the way about the difference between the true false friendships and the friendship-of-which-I-speak. This is impossible without the aid and the grace of the Literature of which I speak, which is the quinte essence of these mixtures of you and of me, in which I can tell you everything without losing myself and without losing you and without our having to demonstrate and explain the mysterious whole of which I speak. You have to take the road. Within. So, arriving at the

Tower with M., and knowing that time was of the essence, life, life – any life – lasting such a short time, had been as long, as often delayed, complicated, put on hold, as our trip to India had required conjunctions of chance and progress in seeking the composition of the mixture friendship–literature. One must go to the Tower as to the Ganges with one's heart prepared, this too is as quinte essential as returning to a native land. One must be ready to receive. So, each time I checked and re-checked everything, as if I consulted the auspices and with the very same meticulousness that I use in revising for my mother the cathedral of her native Strasbourg. One must make sure that on every hearth Peace is lit and on every altar that is in any way connected to the idea of the Tower. I couldn't go to the Tower with O., with the war on. Since I saw no end to the War, having grown aware that it was inextricably entangled with the very source of our encounter, I'd begun, I'd more exactly decided to begin to think that I could not go again to Tower with O. Of course O. himself might well have been thinking the same thing.

*

I could not imagine that I would *never* return to Montaigne, if there is a place to which I am as attached as one is attached to love itself, I mean, for me to literature as life, the way I am attached to my mother, the tower being my literary mother, that place is Montaigne. I couldn't excise literature from my heart. To imagine I would not return to Montaigne was to imagine I wouldn't write, that I would be dead alive, that I would kill my mother my children my cats within me, while continuing to live under my own roof, that I wouldn't answer M. on the telephone (impossible, in fifty years this has never happened), that I would have reached the shores of indifference where I would never again read Kafka, where I could

124

spend years without the desire or the need to drink a drop of Shakespeare, where I could picture my whole body not quivering, when it happened, in a tragedy, upon two diamond words, for which I would deploy weeks, all consecrated to probing them, pondering them, dreaming of them, where I would live as if I had never read a line of Stendhal, where all the libraries by which I breathe would be walled up, where I would forget each instant and each sentence of the days spent in Montaigne with M. and, afterwards, each of his gestures and the singular form of his fingers, totally, where I would be the conscious witness and agent of forgetting, where I would not toss and turn in any feverish suffering, I would feel only the paleness and the distance that comes over the figures of the soul's anemia, was to imagine that I would spend my nights in a coma, that I would drift rigid and vacuum-packed in the folds of an eternal ice sheet, that I would lead an impossible existence in a glacial land where the memory of having been born in a warm country and of having lived would be as distant, strange and ghostly as a memory enrobed in amnesia, to imagine that I would have, how or when I don't know, brought upon myself and deserved a fate as dreadful (seen from here) as that a Dante meted out to the very great innocent criminals or to the incestuous sons.

In a tenth of a second, the impossible becomes possible. It is that *the impossible is possible*.

This is incredible.

I hover for a few minutes over my sleeping mother. Then, making up my mind, as if seeming to yield to fate, and at the same time taking its side (fate's, or my mother's), I head straight for the exit.

One cannot go to Montaigne in an anti-Montaigne state of soul.

July 5, 2010

Once I've really decided to give up Montaigne, therefore to give up the literature-of-which-I-speak, and as if at last having made up my mind to go into exile, as if renouncing literature out of over-faithfulness to literature, I coldly examine the consequences:

So last year was "the last time"? I circle around the theme of "The Last Trip" with all the passion and zeal of a scientist. There are last times by anticipation. This last time appears to be of a different species: "The last time we didn't know was the last time." It took place in a between-time, one of those little dead-end drives I take day after day in my dreams, I think I'll save time by branching off, I exit the human highway, I cut across country, I find myself faced with the same scenario: a cul-de-sac in a rough neighborhood, barred by a wall whose height is absolute. When, after uneasily reversing, I find myself back at the junction with the great human highway, it's as if years had gone by in the space of five minutes, I can't find my old life any more. A whole life has passed; like a piece of flotsam I merge with the strange flow of vehicles and everything is terribly unfamiliar. I am the foreign traveler returning from the country unknown to the other drivers. So, I tell myself, last year we went to Montaigne for the last time without knowing that it was the last time. In a flash, this idea, "the last time," which wasn't the last time up to the hour when The Decision was taken, has become before my very eyes the memory of the last time. The images have retired behind the past's curtain – the lighting dims, the Montaigne scene which was as bright as ever grows dusky. Of course it is not the scene itself which fades, it is the gaze of the grieving spectator that drapes the set in grey tulle. But in another way, I mused, not having known or not knowing the last time was *the* very last time is perhaps a way to circle around death without meeting it.

126

Not-ever-agains in all directions:

Not to be a "*traveller*," no trip, no tower, no return to the tower, no land of no return, no – the last time

Did I know? Or, rather: did you know? Did I have a presentiment? Or rather, did you have a presentiment?

The discretion of presentiments: hadn't you already thought during last summer's pilgrimage "this is surely, or this is perhaps, the last time that we will come to the temple," a thought fleeting, fled, one of me says that, fears that or desires that, no consensus, one doesn't know, the statement is wrapped in wisps of cloud, it takes on the gaseous consistence of a dream, is dispersed by an outburst of buttercups, one tries to decipher the augurs, one becomes a secret soothsayer, the entrails of the year to come are full of disquieting embryos like a cow raped by a gang of furious gods, the threats are multiple and shadowy, desire is enclosed in a stockade guarded by a trembling cortège of vigilantes. Only uncertainty seems certain. From long ago the tender refrain, laden with childhood sorrows, with their sexual connotations, comes back, "we'll to the woods no more the laurels are cut down" we would sing in a vaguely martial tone brows struck by the branches of the bushes that whipped Nerval's cheeks and shoulders, the woods haunt, I thought it a song, it was already the elegy, but cut from its mourning roots, it was the universal prophecy.

At this point, on the dawn of July 5, with the moon for company, I descended, clippers in hand, and I compulsively cut back the wild laurels in the garden, I could no longer stop myself, I did this for no reason, dumbly obeying the clippers. When I came to my senses, that is, to the white paper as figure of my soul, the reason for my gesture showed its wan face at the window of paper. The idea that I went to cut the laurels under hypnosis, having taken orders from the shadow of myself. The first part of the prediction

127

having come true, it followed that we would not go to Montaigne.

Who gave the order to whom? Who put the clippers in my hand? Who gave my right hand the strength to cut despite my arm's paralyzing ache? At that hour, the difficulties: the tohu-bohu from the dozens of aftershocks shaking the house's henceforth magmatic bedrooms, the swirling crater of regrets percolating up in moans and groans from dozens of kilometers below ground, the friction that follows any decision like its bitter twin, a mixture of windy blasts and white fogs descending, abnormally rapid drops in temperature, *for everything is happening in the heart's Antarctic*. Different ways of making the break: not tell O. "I don't want to live with you any more" (start an argument – reconcile, go for a walk, feel guilty, attached, anxious, angry, responsible, suspicious, confident, forced, indebted, afflicted, careworn, invaded, stupefied, indignant, weary) (invaded, possessed, haunted, weighed down, dragged down, for ever). Say: "I'm making a break with Montaigne." It's with myself I am breaking. Consequently with you O. A semi-break, a break via contamination of breaks. The break is full of breaks. One ought to speak of breaks. Breaks break. It breaks. There is adieu. This too one should examine coldly. Hypothesis: what I consider a substitute is perhaps the thing itself. Might it be with me, hence with the writing, that I want to break, so as, hypothesis in the hypothesis, to mourn in advance for all that is me, in anticipation of the Bereavement, the wreck of the *Endurance* of mama, that awaits me at the far edge of the Ice Pack? Not long after, in five minutes the temperature rises from 40 degrees below zero to 11 degrees below, centigrade, as happens in the magellanies. This makes for a strong sensation of warming, for an hour one might think one was in a temperate zone. I suspend all inner motion. Decision: to wait.

In a parenthetical moment between the sudden changes

128

of temperature, I suddenly change tack, stop thinking about "me" and I adopt O's point of view:

She's impossible to live with. She has no respect for O., if he paints a picture, boredom is painted all over H.'s face, she is utterly without interest in the hundreds of photos he wants to show her, she prefers her scraps of paper to any human being; by the same token she can burst into tears over the imagined suffering of some cat, but squeeze out a tear over his own various ills – forget it. Her way of examining O.'s eyes, his burns, his lumbagos, and even the way she clips his toenails is medical, without an iota of emotion or compassion, if she has always come to his rescue in the difficult moments of his life, when it comes to the little things, don't even think about asking her for help; when O. asks her which bus to take, how to book a plane ticket or find an architecture book, to remove a stain from his shirt, you'd think he was taking the bread from her mouth, in all such small instances she employs this dehumanized voice, you'd think her a clerk behind a window in some government office, she has no sympathy for O.'s political enthusiasms, a matter on which she refuses to budge, she is right, he is wrong, her way of reasoning is a form of tyranny, when she enters a room, everyone stops talking, does she notice? No. O. has always adored her, and if he is ready to prove his love, she refuses to call love the very thing O. calls love. She'd rather write than take a walk, and not just with O., but with the entire universe. She is capable of charm but frankly for nothing. Now and then she will smile inscrutably. Once she told O. that she had no difficulty conceiving of making love with sheep, or cats, but never in a hundred years with certain perpetually phallic animals. Even if this was in a dream (one of H.'s dreams, O. doesn't dream) O. felt unspeakable disgust and also that her remark was aimed at him. Her list of things wrong with O. is endless. O. is attached to her as to no one else in the world. Not for this or that reason. And there's the problem. Why be attached to someone you curse every day? O. would like to understand. Everything in the life of the author is a blatant ignoring of O. All her time she devotes to her mother and the rest to her writing. O. doesn't know whether this is a reproach. O. has a great deal of respect and affection for the author's children. He doesn't know in which column to inscribe this fact which seems to go against the fact that she loves only her writing. He starts a column "contradictions," which in a twinkling fills with brouhaha. He starts a column "incomprehensibles" and he closes it immediately, for in truth, everything about this personage is totally incomprehensible. O. has always been able to bear this. O. estimates the proportion of pain and suffering in their relationship at ten percent. This is correct. The rest is fine. When O. thinks about how she wants him to stop smoking around her, he goes crazy with rage. She encroaches upon all his freedoms. Lastly she does not accept O.'s maxim: I am the way I am. He could never have married a person like her. But this is not the question. If, with women, O. naturally needs to be dominant, one can't consider H. as a woman even if she makes frequent use of this word, H. doesn't know what a real man is. When O. begins a sentence with "men," the author tells him: "men, man, what's that? You?" She complicates everything, beginning with everything she says. Even her silences. She has only ever loved poets. O. has never imagined life without knowing that H. was nearby. He wants to kill her but he'd be miserable if she died. If O. could dream, he'd carve her up into bite-sized chunks, then he'd feel better, too bad he never dreams. O. feels very strongly that this is not fair. O. is a good person. He has so much tenderness for hearts of gold.

*

The temperature climbs to 9 degrees below zero, centigrade.

130

To go? Images turn up at the door all out of breath: You will go, they say, tomorrow at daybreak. It was so windy on the staircase I was incapable of predicting what might really happen at dawn the next day. An oscillation of the heart at the end of its tether. I went to O. I said: "We'll go, tomorrow." O., I note, says nothing. I ignored him. Shortly before I had told him: "It is necessary to renounce going to Montaigne." I didn't know what he was thinking. Once promulgated, an hour later, sometimes in the space of a minute, the irreversible reverses itself. Hearts are in delirium's clutch. The firm ice upon which we stand, harassed, gasping for breath, suddenly cracks underfoot, we leap onto a nomadic floe, perhaps we should have chosen the other one, we can't decide, we drift

just then little tornadoes of anguish with sharp hooves, snorting and splashing. Terror of leaving my mother alone? But it's not that. It's the chain of events, the voices drown each other out, soprano and alto, it's the storm, thought thinking in syncopations. Two fears collide:

(1) The fear of the conflict en route, already one hears hell howling on the highway: Smash! Destroy! Gobble! Devour! The vehicle is nothing but a wooden crate. *It had to happen*, I tell myself, I slid to the ground, I heard cars, and O., rumbling, we're going to have an accident I told myself and I'm going to be killed. I tried to keep my head down, just in case. *And it happened.* Smashed, destroyed, the crate of a car in smithereens, splintered contents strewn along the edge of the road. But no one is hurt. Only getting home is problematic. The vision of my mother, an old cat, alone, in the house, with the lamb and the mouse, makes me sob. What mortally saddens me is the fate of my three animals.

(2) The fear of the twin conflict, latent, held down by a compromise one necessarily makes with oneself: no matter what, I must, must race back to my mother's side. And there you have it: the aborted Occasion.

I dread my dreads. I wrestle with my fears. All night the terrified dreams seek a hiding place, a den. Never had the Tower appeared to me so distant, so inaccessible. At 7 in the morning I demand of myself a surplus of courage. In any case, it's a matter of renouncing and of not renouncing. Go. It will be the last time. I tell myself. Think about it: the trip takes two hours. I need to build myself a wall of insensitivity good for five hours, I figured. Drape oneself in an inner patience big enough for the trip there, the trip back, and visiting the Tower itself only takes an hour, one must fashion a mental skiff capable of holding up under a film of ice for a good five hours. I fashioned myself a patience like a museum, its main room modeled on the Montaigne library, which I had no trouble hallucinating.

Visions

The Tower is still and round like a woman asleep on her feet while posing for Rembrandt, like our theater's immobilized ship, its ropes caught in ice, immobilized

Vision: beloved entrails of the Tower. The spiral staircase. Its portrait can be found in Rembrandt's visionary painting, *The Philosopher in Meditation*. What does spiral thought have to tell us? In order to think, one must begin at the bottom of the thought, where impulses and penchants for death simmer. In the beginning it is a good idea for the traveler to pretend to slay the dragon, to frighten it, to chase it away with threats. Next, after having climbed past the celestial cupola, one begins the ascension toward the books. The staircase is so constructed that it prevents any armed confrontation. No one can brandish a sword while climbing, for the stone screw represents an obstacle for the right arm. The philosopher meditates in his sleep.

132

This is the last time, you tell yourself, at 8 in the morning. Right away inauspicious signs:

(1) At 8:30, just before our departure, O. bangs "a gift" – he calls it – down on my desk. A gun. It was in my drawer, O. says.

Death. I thought. But who can say who and how she – *la mort* – is going to kill. O. didn't set the gun down on my desk. He banged it onto the face of the manuscript whose body lies naked on the overpopulated table. It's as if – no, it's not as if.

Now someone dies. But simultaneously one must think: now it is the gun that dies. One may also think: this is an old memory turning itself in. So many things can change object and objective in the space of a minute. Nothing is certain.

O. said: "a gift"! That too can be understood in a dozen different ways. For O. a gift, for H. the sign of an assassination. No one is right in the place of someone else.

I didn't touch the thing. I didn't breathe a word. I "answered" with a mute non-answer. I wanted to go to Montaigne, nothing in the world could have modified my decision at that moment. I left the gun aside for later.

(2) Right after our departure, a kilometer from the house, O. veers onto a side road. We exit the straight and narrow road to the Tower. One feels one's heart ready to leap out the window of its chest in shock and vexation. All my strength has been mustered for a super-fast return, to shorten the torments of my mother, left behind in the uncommunicative solitude of the house. In my view O. is aiming at my mother in me, and at my mother. I say nothing. Later I'll murmur: every-meter-counts. O. then drives so slowly that the cars behind grow impatient, but I don't say a thing. I keep my word, that is, silence. I now turn myself into pure will to see the mission to the end (I can't say to a good end): reach Montaigne, celebrate the rite, don't break the fast, cross the

abysses, don't wake the dragon in the downstairs room, salute the stars and return.

During the crossing
One must not cry out. One can't cry out. Calling mama is as pointless as if she had been lain in the land of the dead. We left her on the other side. One looks at one's watch as if it had something to tell us. One prays. One thinks ceaselessly of the maxim that Montaigne had engraved above his head in the library. *Solum certum nihil esse certi.* The only certitude nothing is certain. We took the risk. Certitude of the uncertain.

Going, I think of the return. Coming back I think: among all the uncertainties a single certitude: I went to Montaigne to try to *save the tie* that binds O. and me together. Having so decided I took the risk of putting my mother in danger. Not for one reason or another. I should not have gone to Montaigne, for this, that or another reason. I couldn't not go to Montaigne, perhaps it is *I couldn't not go to Montaigne for the last time.* To look death in the face? To look life in the face? I couldn't. *I went out of impossibilities.* Not for this reason. Not for that reason.

*

We stayed seventeen minutes in the end, I'd said on the phone: eleven minutes, but in the end I stood in the Ganges for seventeen minutes, and this thanks to the unexpected.

The night before our visit I called the Château office. In the middle of the combat I was waging with myself, I'd found a stratagem in an attempt to perhaps outwit the fates by changing the givens of the calculations on which the unconscious feeds. It was an attempt to get around the barrier of the hours: the Tower only opening to visitors at 11 o'clock I'd come up with an improbable derogation: we'd depart at dawn while my mother was still asleep, or even in the small hours with the stars, this would be the perfect formula, go before daybreak, so everything would take place while my mother slept, she would hear nothing, would not suffer, we'd go like a dream, waking she would already have forgotten. I saw that this did not remove the malevolent weight, the threat of an accident, but at least there was a chance that it would happen as if it had never happened. Therefore I called the Tower, I pleaded my cause warmly, with conviction, sincerity, I stripped my household bare, narrated my centenarian mother in bed, I'd quoted Montaigne quoting Homer, "one can utter many words in one sense and in the other," and all for nothing, yes yes they answered that is to say no no no, this was an impossible impossibility there was no way under the sun to change the opening hours, before 10 in the morning no wheel no hoof passes the barrier, and the Tower itself will not surrender before the eleventh hour, I could be queen king or ghost the Law will not be moved by the emotions of human being, I was in vain. "'To every argument,'" I murmured, "'there is an equal and opposite argument,' it's written on the thirty-eighth beam of the Library," I say. Yes yes no no. I didn't attempt to bribe my way in, I took my human chance. Nothing more.

*

Arriving at 10 in the park, we'll go to the foot of the Tower, I say, and we won't enter, waiting an hour is realistic, but I can enter by heart, I will go and touch his foot stroke his knees, run the tips of my fingers over the crevices, put my lips to his lips and we will leave again. Eleven minutes. Maybe nine. The trip will last four hours and thirty minutes if all goes well. Every time Montaigne went traveling in July, he saw himself taken prisoner by the captains of Paris, lodged in

135

the Bastille, set free at 8 in the evening, the first prison he ever knew, thanks to the Duke of Elbeuf who had him captured by way of reprisals for a gentleman of the Ligue taken prisoner at Rouen. Anything can happen, what inanity in things! "No man has known, nor will know, anything for certain."

The guard informs me for the first time of something I have known for forty years: one does not enter before the stroke of 11. Not for this reason nor for that reason. I say: I will not visit. I tell the truth. I say: I am only going to give the Tower a hug and leave. I have had its interior painted inside me for forty years. I say: as soon I have blessed it, blessed I shall depart. Nothing more. Upon which, *with no reason*, this unknown guard rose, with no explanation *she held out the key of the Tower*.

This is the first time in forty years that I have received the Key to the Tower, with no apparent cause, or legitimacy, not because of this, nor because of that, I am able freely to cross the threshold of the Law, and freely and alone enter the Library in reality. After this forty-year impossibility, freed on the stoke of 10 o'clock in the morning, I felt as I felt when I found without seeking it Kafka's unpublished manuscript, one of the lost versions of "Vor dem Gesetz" whose end was, as I immediately saw, an inversion of the published version, and without any marks to explain its genesis. In this version, which I came upon by series of German chances so extraor-dinary that one day I will try to write the story if I have the strength and time, at Marbrach am Neckar, in 2006, that is to say, not long after the inauguration of the Museum of Modern Literature, a veritable Alexandrian Library, where I'd gone, not at all to consult Kafka's manuscript but, at the invitation of the conservators of the precious collection of manuscripts, two handsome young men, ardent, cultivated, tall, cut out for their roles in a room that I already saw gliding past me in hypermodern form and whose philosophical and mystical contents would echo the revelatory texts of Hoffmann, Hofmannsthal and Hesse, to admire as a connoisseur some handwritten letters of Derrida which these conservators rejoiced in being the guardians of. I'd never seen an edifice as strangely elegant and dreamlike; its two blocks, like two minimalist temples perched on pillars, seemed to be the metamorphosis of two books, upright, open to be read. And the two conservators cut from the same cloth were part of the dream of the archivist architect. There and then, I had the enchanted surprise. Wishing to linger in front of the luminous box in which the sheets of paper in Derrida's hand were displayed, I found myself drawn by one piece of furniture among the hundred that shelter the trial of *The Trial*. I was wearing white gloves, I was alone, I was free, in the room it rained a light from the moon, everything was bathed in the intense silence of the dream, I could hear the ghosts' hearts beating, stirred at the approach of a passionate visit. This is not the place to recount *The Trial*. It is in a slim but large folio that I glimpse, as in a distant theater, the drawings – in Kafka's hand – that obviously illustrate the single scene of "Vor dem Gesetz." I recognize it all. Then the last page. I know it by heart, it seems to me that I am about to put my arms around it. Suddenly, and truly as if in a dream, that's not what it is. This is not how it ends. I don't believe myself! I see – and the last of Kafka's sketches countersigns this, one sees the beggar himself *plunge*, arms wide as if he were swimming or flying in space, pass through the gate which was forever off limits, his whole body gathered into a single wing or tail, rushing in such a movement of *liberation* that I couldn't believe it. For a split second I believe I've dreamt this, I've mixed up the file folders, but I was clasping the volume firmly in my white-gloved hands, I touched it. These pages had infiltrated the hundreds of sheets of paper of the *Trial* folder. A surreptitious play. This can happen. In the bottom right-hand corner of Kafka's lively handwriting, its letters always looking like beings going somewhere, running away, involved in arguments, falling over, doing somersaults, I saw:

I saw and I read.

One enters a temple in order to consult the oracle and it's another god who answers you.

Perhaps in the meantime the two Marbrach angels discovered my discovery. Or vice versa. I left the temple as I left the Tower, in the silence that drapes its dusky silk mantle around any person who has just tumbled into the realm of the sacred. There's nothing one can say.

So there's the secret: *at the end of his life*, the person is allowed to enter at the very moment he has been told it is his fate to remain forever at the door. The door is his door. His personal door, the mirror which takes his image and doesn't give it back, his decree, she holds up her hand and he can read *No* on the palm. The door has from the beginning signified: you shall not enter, you who want to enter. It is the end. One stands in front of one's door. One's body wholly empty. Enter the Unexpected, exit the Expected, the two cross without a word. The poor man doesn't even have time to see the door open, it doesn't even disappear, it has disappeared, a big cool wind has risen, he embarks flat on his stomach on a raft of air, saved. This is *a new twist* I tell myself. I see moreover, in the margin of a sheet where the figures seem to rush forward so as to exit the paper, the word *Umschwung*, underlined.

The event's immensity does not appear to me. Not until I have been back at my point of departure, that is to say at my point of initial oscillation, for some days. One morning, the event rises like a slow sun. Out of the corner of my eye I glimpse the first ray. Only today, while writing, with difficulty, upstream against the flow of time, do I see in the distance, ahead of me, the Event, in all its Light. The events in which we are rolled up like frail puppets pulled hither and thither by the tempests the gods invent only happen to us with a lag in time. It is the poet or author who transforms the ant into a hero. As long as Homer isn't looking at him with his words, Ulysses is a sailor who drifts back and forth in front of the door and whose every initiative is an act of wishful thinking, I tell myself. I noted this on July 10. It is what would have changed "miserable and prideful man" – of whom Montaigne speaks a dozen or more times in sentences that shine over his head and in his heart, that is to say, "man," "man who is nothing," "man whose mind wanders in the shadows and, blind, can't see what is true (*cernere verum*)," "man who presumes (*existimat*) upon his knowledge and doesn't know that he doesn't know (that is to say Ulysses, me, O., you, or you) – into "man" climbing toward the beginning of thought, taking the staircase that winds, by a *spiral* ascension, one must insist, from ordinary disaster to the room where a thousand books are going to speak to him, that is to say a character taken in and welcomed by one Homer, or another, *at the end of his life*, then and only then and on this condition, for after having committed hundreds of errors, having understood nothing, left in one's wake dead friends and abandoned women, *in extremis* one *about-turns* and at the last moment one reflects. At this moment, Homer (or some other Kafka) rushes to open the door and lets one *enter alive*.

*

Successively,
I'd renounced going to Montaigne
Then I'd renounced renouncing going to Montaigne
I'd renounced entering the Tower
I'd renounced appealing

I had felt neither revolt nor regret

All of a sudden – I had the key in my hand, a big old key, with a string looped through the hole in its head, and nothing or no one rose up between the possibility of entering the Tower, unconditionally, of entering The Law from outside the law – and me

I found myself in the Tower.

I was alone with her, in her, in the most beautiful and profound solitude in the world, extra-temporally. I stood in a column of light. Words were singing. The girl who had held out the Key-without-explanation had granted me not only the instrument, but also forgetting and freedom. Neither followed nor supervised me. In this dream in reality, she acted like the mythological genius of the Tower. She granted desires before I'd even had to think of them. She wore a black slip of a dress with straps that revealed the slightly soiled white straps of her bra. And a natural, unforced smile. The idea that she was an innocent or a spirit didn't come to me. The idea that she was of the same species as the two library angels at the Marbrach portico – didn't come to me. The idea that it is absolutely forbidden to give the Key to a visitor and for a visitor to touch the Key – didn't come to me.

I entered the Tower *for the first time* in my long history of towers. Up to now I had been admitted. (Preceded, authorized, controlled.) I was there and it was as if I was at home there. As I would have been in my writing mill. As if I were moving from room to room *just as usual*. I went around quickly, I recorded, I stored in my mind each piece of wall of this place I had kept myself outside of for forty years, I took in the saint and the dragon. They had been unveiled. I took them in one piece, posing in front of each lens, facing the spectator, I didn't waste a star or a blazon. I climbed quickly, the spiral shod me, we are old friends I tell myself, I had the

140

quick and rapid foot of ownership, I darted looks in all directions, I was someone other than the reserved visitor, looking from side to side, restraining her impulse to press up against the wall, to sit down on the prie-dieu, who I had been, so it seemed, for centuries, the year 1571 was at the window which gave on the garden, I savored for a long time the act of mourning upon which Montaigne had founded his work, and upon which he laid the votive act.

They'd cleaned and brightened up the walls for me, I noted, nothing escaped my faithful tour of inspection. I loved the tower as Michael Montanus loved Stephanus Boetius dulcissimus suavissimusq. when at last he was able to give body to his desire, even the stairs, each of them worn in its own way, I brushed with my feet like my own teeth. I was the subject of an act of grace, I was in another time, all repose and leisure. All this happened "in reality." Had I been able to think, I might have feared or suspected that the price of this grace was my condemnation to perpetual exile, but no thought was able to scratch the purity of this totally unspoiled (*integer*) moment. Simplicity bathed the whole of my redoubt's interior in filtered light. My head bent, eyes brimming with the return of time past, I murmured rapid phrases to those who kept me company in my concrete ecstasy, to my dead kept living, to little children, to the poets, to the cats, to my father, to my near and dear who, like Montaigne's very gentle, very suave very closely allied and super-elect, are expert in telepathic communication. In the bedchamber, near the praying apparatus, I called "Balzac!" and right away the cat was there. It suffices that I say his name once a year, into the telephone that the Tower also is, and instantly he enters. Cats having so little time to endure, I have never seen Balzac come in without thinking joyfully and mournfully, "Balzac is still here." True cat that he is, he is merely still-there. The loyalty between Balzac and me is powerful and sober. This creature is the proof of the solidarity of spiritual and fleshly ties which, when they exist, make the world of finalities an empire charitable to souls. He is the-once-a-year-cat, the cat by alliance, the catgod, delegate to the occult life of beings who nourish friendship with communication. What invests Balzac Montanus with the strange and fateful gleam of tragic heroes is that the Balzac motif finds itself situated in the center of a vast carpet of time whose fabrics, silks, remnants are woven at different epochs but within the agitated tale that I am trying to collect in a single volume, certain parts of this weaving coming from those Antarctic years in which one of my memories is kept in an ice palace, others belonging to diverse future times whose figures are even brighter than certain traces of past scenes. When I see Balzac, I see the cat that wants to play, that leaps onto the Library table and into the *Essays*, one before or after the other

As I was stroking Balzac who rolled onto his side to be totally anointed with touching, simultaneously I was saddened to think that no later than tomorrowalreadyhere my fingers would be grazing the skeleton, which caused my eyelids to redden with tears already, and crouching as I was, my knee on the small gravel of the meadow, inside myself I descended the tower staircase with its worn steps which is exactly the same as the spiral staircase darkly brushed with crimson by which Rembrandt leads us for eternity into the thoracic cavity of philosophy. And a little further to the left, in the austral half of my heart, I was present during the laying in the ice of the cat Anatole who perishes mourned by the whole crew of *Endurance*, united like a single father around the small curled-up body of their collective child.

Here I took note that I will have to try as often as necessary to accept the mental panic attacks that blow up suddenly in my throat and at the back of my forehead, for each time such an attack is launched, at first I sink, or so I am convinced.

Then after a few hours, sometimes a few minutes, one pulls oneself up again with the quasi-magical celerity of a muon.

One never gets used to these lightning blows, there's no time. They are caused by the *interpolation* of times. The interpolation becomes a psychic substance, a neurological terrain where the lavas of distant and still fluid periods mingle. The word *interpolation* could be the title of a blinding-white narrative of the planet's so-called zones "of the beyond" by one of those archi-genial explorers who serve me as uncles of controlled delirium, given that from the start of the twentieth century they buzzed around the South Pole's skull like archangels attracted by the undefiled crown. Or the name of one of those ships refitted and transformed from seal hunter into super-vessel destined for the superhuman Antarctic exploit via a series of transplants and encrustations that grind the hull down into a sort of battered coffer scratched and scarred something like the manuscript found in a bottle containing the tale of a shipwreck of which only the tale remains. *Interpolation* (the name of Ulysses' ship when he himself was called Nobody), a cunning, glorious name, which reminds us how the power of the truth is folded into a fabric woven of beat-up, mingled, weary, lifted-up and resuscitated times.

The ship is refitted to the point of appearing in the guise of a totally unpublished subject. But it is endowed with secret energies whose imperceptible vibrations the passengers sense, through the survival in its flanks of a ghostly treasure.

At 10:37 I launched the maneuver of detachment. I moved off backwards, face turned toward the Tower, counting each step, I wasn't moving, I was standing on time's quay, the Tower drew away from the edge of my life as slowly as the Ship whose dream of the beyond of the beyond of the known lands, toward which it now turns, makes it shine. Everyone, on the quay as on the boat, thinks of and begins a conversation

143

with death. Let me pass, someone says. Someone smiles. The smiles shine.

I call this backing away *an adieu without adieu*: one doesn't cut oneself off, one doesn't turn one's back, one moves away keeping one's eyes on the adored object, one enters the moving away, the moving away is an immense continent, one is going to live a long time, one doesn't know how long, in the moving away, the heart beats grief's uncertainties. One addresses words full of passion to the face that slowly withdraws toward the depths of time, useless and magical scraps of advice – "don't forget me," "look after us," "you know" – the stammerings of faith, to the visage whose dimensions little by little grow more tenuous, which becomes a figure. Cedar branches come to cover the cheeks of the Tower like hands raised to conceal anxiety's blinking, one believes one sees a sadness, now the figure enters the unreality of memory, now the Tower grows bigger, gathers itself into a fragment that rises to cover the whole height of the field of vision, it's the whole upper part of the edifice with its narrow eyes, its rounded forehead, and on its head the little hat, which expands, carried by the strange power of synecdoche. Never will the Tower have appeared to us so important so grave, so imposing and consenting, as in these last moments. She is in pale gold, she looks at us with the resigned compassion of a mother who knows that abandon awaits us and what abandon has in store.

This is the end of childhood. Until, through the mildest of slippages toward the glowing, mysterious depths of time, the visage, as indistinct now as that of the meditating philosopher, sharpens in the frame that awaited it. One click and it changes to memory. Now the Tower is fixed. Changed into soul, like those dear persons with whose beings we converse in dreams, and whose absence of fleshly appearance doesn't stop us meeting them with emotion. At this moment, one ceases breathing. She is painted.

Part III

PEACE!

On my desk, as I was saying my last farewell, the gun had grown to the size of a wooden box big enough to hide all my papers, and which I saw as if from a great distance, like a phantasmagoria, but real and in my study, the room itself dilated by the presence of this object, situated by the illusion some thirty meters from my chest. Instead of the Tower, the gun. I blinked the apparition away, it retreated slowly, giving me time to recognize a coffin's outlines.

*

Yesterday evening, back from the expedition, all I could think about was the past that had just taken place, about the Tower in the past, about the endless future of the past. I was tempted to displace the gun scene. This is not a fiction. It was July 7. With the help of Courage, a secondary but pivotal character, I executed an about-face, I repressed a powerful urge to flee, certain that the disarmament attempt was reasonably bound to fail. Attempt to bring up with my bare hands a fragment of fossilized unconsciousness encrusted in the bottom of a vertiginous quarry carved into a rectangular volume two hundred square meters in circumference and forty meters deep – that's what awaited me. I looked everywhere for a way to get to the bottom of this huge sand-colored pit. One sees the fossils clearly. After all, they are no more than a hundred breaststrokes away, although they date from the most archaic periods of our species. I saw no stairs, no ladder, not on this side nor on that, nor can one imagine climbing such a vertical and brittle wall. I'm going to have to call the fire brigade, I tell myself. Become a helicopter. As soon as I had made up my mind to attempt the dive, I came up against all the most insignificant obstacles, resistances, series of mishaps. At the very moment when, not heeding my hesitation, I head for O. (he sits at his HQ, the yellow garden table, puffing on a cigarette), obeying instinct, he draws himself up to his full height, and exits stage left with feet of stone. I wanted to make a beeline for him, shout: "O.!" etc.

Instead of making a beeline for O., I went out onto the balcony, I carried my mother in my arms, I installed her in the nest of an armchair and I offered her suitably distracting objects, which I laid out, within reach, on the table covered with the oilcloth whose bright stripes she is fond of. Here are the vegetable she likes to dominate, a pound of green beans, to which I'd added some painted vegetables, a brainwave I'd had. While she nipped the tails off the beans with the rosy pink scissors, I meant to talk to her about the painted vegetables' other deep and mysterious life. "We are going to do some chardining," I say. I'd made myself a festive group of peaches and pears. I kept the asparagus for the last act. With her five hundred green beans my mother had a motherlode

148

Meanwhile I follow O. inside – one acts the colossus, one exits like a statue, one says, "So long, you won't be seeing me again," and one gets no further than the first landing in the altercations between members of a same family, this false exit, because it is false, allows the character to produce an outburst whose appearance is frightening. Insofar as one has the vague sense that the ties of clan or peoples are by definition unbreakable, one can on the one hand intensify the violence, on the other one has a desperate urge to let oneself go, commensurate with the impossibility of severing blood ties. These invisible ties are the most frequent causes of murders; to purge these poisoned veins, it would be necessary to carry out a total exsanguino-transfusion, with no guarantee that this purgation would enable the vital disentanglement.

"O!" I cried, I imagined. It would be like planting my cry in the gills of some great fish, a blind sea monster living five hundred meters below the surface forever contemporary with the primitive epochs of our ancient childhood. I had only five minutes to waste. I was going to gather all my strength into a very fast very brief allocution. This gave the scene, which I perceived in a burning second, the dimensions of a minuscule confessional box. Confess it all, I told myself. To me this felt like puncturing an abscess. I saw H. and O. side by side in a double trance. Each of the plaintiffs addresses the audience with an exaltation doubled by the other exaltation. Their beautiful voices strike and strike. Hate howls in the tones of love enraged, nothing can assuage it. Let's tear ourselves apart equally. In the blackness of the deep, everything is teeth, the whole body is but a gummy tissue of jaws equipped with hundreds of dental thorns. Scour the rocks. Crush the bodies on the spiny reefs. Wearing nothing but shirts, the same shirt, for O. has helped himself to one of H.'s shirts and it just happens to be a shirt of M.'s, that M. gave out of love to H.,

149

which causes H. to bellow with unappeasable wrath. Legs are striped. H. feels ready to expire under the grinding stone, all she has left to assure her survival is a hair-thin crack in the stone of the teeth through which to gasp for breath. Let's not exaggerate. The only prey in O.'s jaws is H. H. shouts that O. has H. permanently clamped in his jaws. The end is nigh. Let's not push it away. One can no longer believe the tie will endure. "I want to LIVE," shouts the one. The other feels unbearable pain at hearing her own words ripped off, stolen from her very own flesh. Calm down, time for a breather and to emphasize the force of the demand: "I demand my rights." My? What my? The other has the right too. The other also wants to live! The lout wants to kill. Everything I say about you stands for me too. When one thinks of these dreadful vomit-like dialogues over the years, skins sold for a penny, crises of despair fed on potatoes, rotten to the melons, you took the piece of cardboard I was going to use, my heart was aching, where did you put the keys to the car? The minute you lose something it's me who lost it, didn't you hear mama ringing? I didn't hear because I was shaving, can't you shave and hear? You always want more and better, everything always, what a relief to hear oneself spit out these scalding phrases one has chewed on for years, burning one's tongue so as, pointlessly, to avoid wounding the other, pointlessly, because whatever one doesn't spit out in one way, one spits out in another, I won't tell you what I think of you, everyone thinks what I think of you, especially your friends and family, they say, I won't tell you, they say, and they say it, pointlessly, because what one thinks of the other is what the other thinks of the other too, finally in sight of the Pole, even if we were to die, they say, it's time to tell one another the pure worst, no admixture, the truth that bites, so H. says, then O. says, and H. tells O. she is perfectly aware what O. told everybody, but she doesn't want to hear about it, for they each take the whole world as witness and hence as hostage says the one, and says the other the same. Together they address the audience, each describes the other, bitterly each one offers as true an image almost entirely false of the other. There's no lack of material, each is in possession of a bagful of munitions dating back to the sixties, the fifties, each sometimes steals some grotesque, vile, disagreeable, totally fabricated anecdote with enormous destructive power, "proof," says O., "symptoms," says H., gradually the lights dim, one descends via insults and insulting reactions to the increasingly baser insult, so one spirals down to the deepest depths where one sees nothing any more, at five hundred meters under the surface one strikes out blindly, one is surrounded by the dense black water of the abyss, and with the pressure one's whole being grows stronger and stronger, smaller and smaller, longer and longer, deformed, soft, soon one is nothing but an almost still pocket of monstrous energy, one has adapted to the unlimited hostilities we necessarily develop when we reach this level of pressure and darkness, each becomes finally a maw bristling with hundreds of antenna-teeth, one is nothing but teeth that see only their prey, that wait and watch, that bristle in the gigantic circle of the jaw, so that the other monster cannot avoid, should it budge, finding itself all of a sudden trapped by the hundreds of teeth with eyes, and clack! but since each of them is made of palings more or less equally mortal, nature produces an instinct of self-defense, so that in the dark, and according to the immune system's principle of deterrence, two monster silhouettes are frozen in a dantesque face to face the way a gaping saccopharynx halts a few dozen centimeters from a sea devil's impending gulp. The spectators perceive only the atrocious, almost motionless struggle for a few seconds at a time when one of the two abyssal enemies emits an infinitesimal bioluminescence, one of those all but imperceptible blinks of light that bacteria in their death urges produce, that swarm in

151

their heads, and it is the very brevity of this vision of horror that makes the audience tremble with dread, for one can only *recognize*, seeing these two petrified terrors, that this is how, on the ocean floor, true hell will open, in the gloom under the gloom. At these depths there is naturally no life possible for the just person, or for lucidity, or even for memory. As for the words that ooze from between all these needles of teeth, they are gibberish. One ends with a blood-streaked, chopped-up soundtrack, from which one picks out shreds of insults, ghostly traces of accusations, syncope battles in the shadows, ellipses' ululations

. . . nth time . . . nth stupidit . . . tter crap . . . 's a mess. I heard . . . rasite, and the testa- . . . what, me? . . . from grandpa's factory . . . azy. But I'm . . . -dulgent. Which way to turn? Get help! And my closest . . . ha! ha! ha! . . . on you? . . . M.'s idea. So go ask him, M. arrogance. I live quietly, with nobody such . . . avarice. I dreamt . . . sordid . . . your landscape of buttocks and breasts . . . get in the way of my work, no, the . . . to nothing . . . the word is jealousy. Me? . . . the most alien of those close to me, the horror of the close . . . your gibberish . . . acknowledge me, except you.

This is when one hears, rising from behind, stage right, an arioso – a contralto voice singing a heart-wrenching lament interrupted by empty silences, whose notes, resonating in diminished fourths, will echo without cease above the voice – evocation of the Song of Songs, from the woman departing in search of the Friend, which is to say the figure of peace and of the fragility of fidelity.

"Oh! my peace has gone! I want Peace, Peace, enough of this din, I want the end, I want the vast, cool silences like the still virgin tablecloths before the party begins, I want the dream walks accompanied by the sea's silvery blue calm – sobs the voice – I want the night starred with childhood's laughing milk teeth at the teats of daylight, I want the beauteous peace that subdues murders."

Weeping *"Peace! Peace! Give me peace! Come!"* one comes to believe one sees suspended overhead (a delightful canvas that descends as if miraculously from the flies) a still flight of four- or six-winged beings (later one will see that they constitute the bewitching, polychrome response to the sea monsters), hovering and swaying to and fro above the garden's trees, the wings in all different pastels like doves', that deploy their dozens of wing models, each more delicate and audacious than the last, in the vast damp blue bowl of the sky. In this full bowl of sky some will recognize the twin of the small sky which, on the ground floor of the Tower, unfolds its sleepy corolla in the shadows over the eternal battle of the saint and the dragon. Sometimes the two characters trade faces. All of a sudden the dragon has the saint's resolute, round face and the saint has the naïvely ferocious mask of the dragon who is trying hard. Each time the saint turns his round face toward me, and not toward the dragon, I've thought, when I was waiting in the lists, I am therefore in the dragon's place, the dragon is me. The round eyes are astonished this goes on for so long, this battle, so long.

He is as young as ever, I am beginning to tell myself, it was the saint I meant,

(my mother picked up the green beans one by one, she tried hard to hold each bean by the waist, aimed the scissors at the being, snipping now the head now the tail, now with an instinct which remains to me inscrutable, she cuts the tail first then the head. Then she tossed the lifeless bean onto the tray. I wasn't helping. The execution of the beans would take an hour. "Stop, if you're tired," I say. But I saw in her eyes that she would go on holding fate's scissors in this way right to the last bean. Each living bean's life is a battle I tell myself)

I was thinking of the saint, and at the same time of Montaigne, of M. also, and I realized that I had always, without giving it much thought, aligned myself with the M.'s,

I had always seen myself with saint or even as saint, always I raised my sword and defended my right, the right of the saint, and it is at this moment – at this moment detached from my personal time by my mother's scissors, taken from my consecrated time, and attached to my mother's completely different temporality – that I realized that in the heat of battle everything is exchangeable, every being changes into every other being, he or it is forever as young as ever, but who or what? The battle, the saint, the knight, the dragon, as if "he" or "it" was but a single being with a burning desire to live, and tied by the struggle to the other actor without whom there is no stage and no scene. No saint without dragon, no dragon without its saint, no saint without dragon at its breast, no dragon that doesn't dream of sainthood. Clack!

From far away a stern expression comes to paint itself on my mother's face. "Who are you thinking about?" I say. My mother chooses a bean, reflects, and cuts off its head. Then the tail.

Meanwhile Peace with its flight as fine as a razor's edge hovers almost invisible among the winged beings, suspended, supplicated, unsure of outcome. Last year, going into the divine closet off the bedchamber, where Montaigne used to crouch and pray, releasing his amens from top and bottom through one hole symmetrical to the other conduit, that of the latrines, I disturbed a bat, it drew a line as fine as a steel thread under my nose. I naturally thought it was my soul fleeing. "We'll go no more to Montaigne, because of O., and for O." Clack!

That's when I heard the door bang, then the words: "I'm leaving!" Or the words: "I'm leaving!" then the door, I'm not sure which. Slammed, as if the door itself had shouted: *I'M LEAVING! BANG! LEAVING!* Everything is in the *B*! It's the word *B*/(ANG) that fascinates me. By the *B*! (...) it's already over. The (ANG) is the echo.

154

There was a shot on the staircase. *BANG!*

G/one! One is pierced by the bullet before one perceives the shot. It'd already gone off. By the time we take note of what's happening it's already finished.

This is how reality happens before one knows it. All by itself. A gun goes off. One has an explosion *in* the barrel. The cartridge explodes in the barrel, and it's the explosion that propels the bullet toward the door. It'd already gone off. – What's going on? What's that noise? My mother said, waving a bean.

– O. left.

– All by himself?

He departed with his army, and he took the Tower with him. I didn't say that.

I felt *relief.* As when a burn suddenly stops smarting. The strange icy relief that follows despair.

(In the heat of the blow all the actors are strewn on the ocean floor, in the positions the truth of the depths has thrown them into. They lie enlaced, this one's head on that one's knees. The maw that was so dreadful to behold now hangs slack, a defused limp rag.)

In my play the scene mounts rapidly toward humanity's happiness, my Archduke already sees the new world awaken attentive, smiling, with dreamy eyes, absorbed in bold constructions, in which initiates will recognize Rimbaud's predictions come true, one would say a natural cathedral whose cloud naves are ribbed in rose and blue, to begin with it looks a little like the Museum of the Marbach Archives, then the Temple of Humanity as Jaurès envisioned it in a dream, as he writes in his journal. He is so *exalted* that the public *sees* it go up as in a grandiose mute film from the beginnings of cinematography, his dream is *realized* with invisible cords, a passage from Dvorak's Ninth Symphony excites enthusiasm and everyone on the stage and in the hall recovers an emotion they haven't felt since childhood, the excited belief in human grandeur, and the delicious force that sees in a rose petal a ship of the air, and in an asparagus stalk the moiré seductions of a shell of rose-grey ribbon coming from a remnant of silk lying in Whistler's studio. Such bliss to attain paradise in reality!

BANG! At this moment, and always at such supreme moments, shots, three, one, I no longer know. Whaa? cries the audience. Whaa? One can't stop oneself. One so wished to believe in it.

Believe-in-it! Such a commotion! But, like all the Icaruses, Believe-in-it has fallen. Some claim the archduke killed himself. But in *my* play, *my* Archduke would never have done such a thing. He was killed. The instrument is blind. The eye that explodes before it thinks. The killer himself. The blind shoot and it's The End of the World. The mirrors and the celestial echoes brim with tears.

The Temple of Humanity was dwindling into the distance, the sky had been yanked down, the audience saw what the dying see in their last moments. And then the pink and blue cathedral shriveled into a dull grey, it sank and rolled over on its side like a ship wrecked in the dark depths of a tumultuous sea on a little canvas almost completely in the shadows, at last it turned all of a sudden into an upside-down shell like a face already dead, turned toward the sky, expressionless. The scene's last action was a summary of all the mythological farewells. I myself could never see it acted, this last scene, that we called *The Adieu*, without tears in my eyes. Each time the last little monument, which up to then was so gay and now was skeletal, and lifting bony, useless arms, departed, I was quick to weep. However, during The Adieu at the Tower, which happened but once, I hadn't wept.

Twists and Turns

No sooner has O. at last left than I feel real chagrin.

Can't deny it. The thing one had dreamt of for months, years, sometimes (of course dreaming is not exactly wanting, I tell myself, dreaming is the pleasure without paying the price for it), this absolutely vital separation for which one had fought, endured four years of war, a siege or three, innumerable strongholds dismantled, I'd given up writing, and I'd given up my Tower which is more myself than myself, I'd touched the bottom of despair, seen clearly announced the disaster of my destiny as projected and set in motion by O., all of me would be destroyed, not just the books that I would no longer write, but my most sacred past, my delicate and religious love for M., the sublime purity of my time alone with my children, everything, except for my mother, who would remain unscathed, wholly nestled as she is in my body, everything that concerns me and is my strength and my secret would quite simply be infiltrated by the potions of reduction and distortion, I believed, but no sooner had I run through these goyesque visions with the help of my imagination, gifted as it is for misfortune, than the atrocities dissipated, a kind of inner good weather returned, a storm-washed sky replaced the excremental daubings, and just as I had lain down, limbs fractured, head in a mist of black grief, on a mattress of blood-stained, sweated- and slobbered-on manuscript sheets, with *but a single idea, die,* the radical simplification, in an eye-blink I was hauled from the infernal muck, sucked toward the heights, scrubbed clean of the demoniac din.

Just as one may go in a flash from bliss to the trespassing of bliss, similarly, drowned, one may pop up like a cork to the sweet light of ordinary life.

Which is what happens. Not for this reason, nor for that. It's Hell, I say, and the next day I feel nothing. It was Hell to the point that I believed it eternal. Which wasn't true. One believes one has touched the bottom of one's own heart: wrong. Another heart beats differently above the heart's double ceiling. As soon as O. had departed, as soon as O. was on the point of departure. Already, accompanying him to the station, I felt real grief take the place of O.

Children! We're all of us children, I tell myself. Upon which I bid farewell to O. The feeling that he is six years old. My mother too.

Twists and turns. Everything twists and turns.

At these words, I felt a book that would call itself *Twists and Turns,* were I able to write it, breathe. I reached for a notebook. Right then I thought: the minute O. left the book came. Then: I'm going to miss O. And at the same time: I can't tell O. I'm going to miss him. Everything re-turns. I carried the green beans, plucked by my mother, into the kitchen.

*

Chapter one of *Twists and Turns* would be: "Mama's Asparagus." I could already picture it. Mama is installed in her chair, facing Manet's *Asparagus*. She is presented with the asparagus as it has emerged from art, before the first representation, naked, unbound, nameless, without signature, without explanation. I wanted to return with my mother to "the origin" of the work of art, that is to say, to the secret spring in which reality bathes so as to emerge streaming with spiritual light. Not the asparagus, but the thing that precedes it.

My mother in front of the asparagus. My mother seated. The asparagus reclining. In the background a ripple of sandy hues, day dawns. One is not sure what exactly. The asparagus points toward my mother. One is nature, the other extremely clothed. In the scene, my mother will be carried away by curiosity, uncertainty, disgust, perplexity. This mixture gives rise to a flow of words that hop and skip about as if to an absurd tune by Satie. A spontaneous, natural pastiche. The spectators, if one has been careful *not to name* the *a*(sparagus), will be just as mystified but less pure than my mother. The extraordinary charm of the object *a* and its enigmatic force are snuffed out the second one pins the butterfly down and nails the thing to the wall.

Let's preserve the *impromptu*. What is so delightful about an impromptu is the actor's innocence. It is always the first morning of the world. One must enter the scene without opinions, without prejudices, without knowledge, without ideas, with the passionate ignorance of a little child, so as to find oneself at the origin of the marvelous. One encounters. Then everything *emerges* for the first time. It is thanks to this inaugural consent that we'll have been able to see the narrator's Françoise pluck the asparagus just as the Felicity of "A Simple Heart" will have been borne heavenward by the sapphire-blue plumage of her parrot. The painter too sees the asparagus's feathers. Naturally, in the beginning of the world, things are still free, names haven't yet hobbled their movements. They are not classified, put into groups, packaged in a concept of species or race, not bundled, not tied up or choked off, they still have their wings, their feet and their breath, they spring, they gurgle bright sounds, they asperge, they grow bigger, all the while bubbling with laughter.

MY MOTHER (wearing a shawl in shades of beige and grey, tinged with ochre, tip of her nose poking like a beak from beneath a beige cap's visor, which gives her a bird's head, for a long time studies the inert reclining asparagus, its head turned toward the head of my mother). – What sort of beast have we here? Is it an animal? But it's – a fish! A fish? *(She looks from me to "the fish.")* But yes! You might think. *(She points.)* Here, a big mouth. Why is the mouth open? *(The asparagus holds still, teeth out of sight.)* It's bizarre. I don't get it. Yes? No? Is it a hand? It's so long! It's a mystery. A bird? *(She looks at me. She removes her glasses.)* Without my glasses I see a sort of muzzle. But I don't understand what of! I don't know what it's doing here. *(Looks.)* Is not beautiful. Yes? Beautiful? No. Don't understand it at all. But there, there are three fingers. No! It is not beautiful. But – is it a fish? *(I burst out laughing. This thing is the undecidable itself, laid – on what? My mother tries to decide, scanning the sheet of paper, on which the asparagus has been reproduced, suspiciously.)* Laid? As you like! But darned if I know what it's doing there on the ground? Poor thing! And that, this, background that one doesn't know what it is, sky, earth, and over there the poor thing with its mouth open. *(She prefers to look at the magnolia. Comes back to the thing.)* I don't know if that's the tail. *(She looks up at me, quizzes me. I don't answer. The asparagus pricks up its head.)* Is it lifting its head? You aren't going to tell me

160

that's a somebody lying there! You don't mean to say it's a bird? Now I see a beak. But with gigantic feathers. A bird amazed by the length of its train. I've never seen such a bird. So maybe a fish. It could be a man's head! But how? He was swallowed by the fish? But how could he get inside the fish? So this fish ate a man? Who poked out his head? Not a pleasant thought! It scares me! I see a fish and it ate a man starting with the feet, that's all. I have no idea how he did it! Do you get it? – Yes, I say. Differently. – Differently? My mother is indignant. I see the fish that swallowed the fellow. His head sticking out. But what's this story all about? He saved his head, but the rest, forget it! – What about the colors? I say.

My mother refuses to answer. So I show her *A Bunch of Asparagus*, copied from a reproduction.

ME. – How about this? – That, my mother says, is a bunch of asparagus! *ME*. – It's a painting. *MY MOTHER*. – A painting? What do you expect me to do with that? Can you peel them? No. They look real enough. Is that something old? It is a bunch of asparagus. Fine. Who'd ever want such a picture? I am not the least bit interested. It's well done. But can you eat it? *ME*. – You wouldn't like to have this painting in your house? *MY MOTHER*. – You can say that again! Why would I put asparagus on the wall? That's kitchen stuff.

Now I show her the *Asparagus* again. Will she grasp the relationship between the one and the many? My mother has advanced in her research:

MY MOTHER. – Aha! This one is coming out of the shark. Interesting: this one was eaten by this shark. But it is coming out. It looks as if the fish is giving birth. To a man. – It's a shark? – Well, it's not a sole, that's for sure. It's a shark, to be so big. It gives me the creeps. The shark swallowed the man but not completely. You always have pictures with people

161

getting swallowed. – There's a name, under the picture, I say. *(My mother reads:)* The Asparagus. There's a shark in the asparagus. I don't know anything about sea asparagus! Still, it's on land. You're going to spoil my appetite! *ME.* – I'll tell you a secret. *(I tell her the secret.)* *MY MOTHER.* – Manet? An asparagus stalk, you say! *ME.* – Sitting on an infinitized table, a table earth, sea, sky, but still a table. What is troubling, that is to say beautiful, is the variety in the unity. The effacing of all demarcations, I say. A table that stretches into sky, an asparagus-lizard that climbs onto the table, half on the table half on a swath of color, askew, ready to fall off. Plus the asparagus is lifting its head. It's not an asparagus stalk, it's a penis lying there twitching its nose. It's not that. It's an iguana. But it's not that. I tell myself. This thing-being, undeniably animated, which veers from one genre to another species, this crocodile, this bird, this half-eaten, half-saved thing, this head that pokes from a ground undecidably sand, this ear of wheat which shades insensibly down to the foot, or conversely that straightens right up to the crown, stayed with me all summer. The day of my arrival in the house I posted it on the section of wall that becomes my painting gallery when I write. I'd obeyed without argument a strong feeling of admiration. This thing could be anything and everything, in turn, could be a tower lying on its side and – And – the ghostly, unexpected and compelling figure of the image, the one and only one, from which I am never separated when I go off on an expedition, for it is for me the *Incarnation* of the Triumph of Life over Death thanks to art's sleights of hand. What does art do when it paints a story? Art goes down to muck about in hell to bring a dead person to life. The unique magic image is the presence, in the same dimensions as the original of the *Dog* Goya recalled from hell, which lifts its head from the subterranean nothingness, and which is *us* crushed between the teeth of infinities but alive, a little hazelnut, its hopeful snout in the jaws of Time. *The dog with its asparagus head*, I was thinking.

*

Chapter one of *Twists and Turns* would have ended with "The Expeditious Impromptu of July 8." *Me.* – What do you think of this picture? *O.* – The asparagus? Nothing. It's an asparagus. That's all. *ME (downcast).* – That's all? *O.* – What? It's a masterpiece? I am not impressed. *ME (pleading).* – A Manet. *O.* – Manet? *ME.* – *(silence).* *O.* – Ah! It's Manet! Sacred Manet!

*

On the endless staircase that suddenly turns into a tunnel then winds toward the edge of a cliff then, in a new twist, descends a few steps, broken old Eurydice follows me step by step, I have my mother at my back – mentally I can see her dusky down-at-the-heels blue slippers flapping around her puffy ankles with their mauve marblings – I think: if she stumbles – I walk bent, braced to receive Old Eurydice collapsing onto my back, I envisage the collapse, one step I think "collapse," the word calls up the ship, the ropes, the coast, how far we are, I tell myself, far from a coast, far from a port, far from a door, and in the slow anxious horizonless journey I sense my mother behind me her face changing at each turn of the screw, each step is the equivalent of a decade I tell myself, I don't turn around, mindful of the collapse, I must not let go of the lifeline, if broken old Eurydice takes a tumble on one of the steps that I have just painstakingly traced out, betrayed by her slippers into which my mother has been metamorphosed (slippers deserving the same astonished admiration as the asparagus, I tell myself. They have something unique, inimitable about them. I call them: the painter's challenge. How to describe them? This parakeet blue that mauves toward the fish's head, this cut softened by time but which finds again at times something like the firmness of a smile and which must evoke for us the instability of mama's indescribable mouth – an opening totally unrecognizable but from which a rich mixture of laughter and syllables comes, and in which one perceives in the dark cavity in the back on the right the fossil of a tooth. This was once a mouth. I imagine the slippers, as they shuffle, exaggerating their idleness, suggesting to my mother that she drop everything. Faithful and perverse, they say let's stop here. And my mother: – I'm too old, I'm going to stop here. – You're listening to your slippers again, I say. Let them grumble and get a move on, I say. How well they express the downside! We are not going to listen to them). One step, suddenly she sags, her whole too-powerful weight falls against my insufficient weight, one doesn't know how heavy the body of an old woman who drops everything is, my right arm snaps, with a loud heavy cry and a rattling of bones, the last couple is felled. I push this picture of things off toward the wall, I grip the banister and I move on, I descend the way one climbs keeping in front of my mother's body the most tenacious, the most stubborn of shields, for what saves broken old Eurydice from collapse is the sight of the back of her daughter to whom she has entrusted every care for her survival. One shifts into low gear: each step can be broken down into at least twenty separate movements of the muscles or joints, one advances in a slow motion calculated to the millimeter, the slipper feels its way over the step's edge with numerous little movements of its head, chooses, slowly lowers its nose, lands, stops, relishes the peace that follows the effort. One rests. One raises one's head. One looks at the walls of the cage. One notices for the first time that the small stretch of red wall under the staircase vault is speckled with white. – Is that new? broken old Eurydice asks in surprise. – It's old, I say. It's always been there. But in the old days we never had time to look. Since my mother has grown so old we see all the things we never used to see. At each step I myself have time to think of churches, wars, paintings and what I should do about O. Perhaps on the next step, I go into a temple whose stairs are replicas of our staircase and, on the tenth step, I have time to compare a red corridor of Tibetan Buddhism with a corridor of a San Marco convent, also red, while the invertebrate couple we form mamame wends its way from misstep to recovery.

– And now what do we do? says my mother behind me. – We keep going down, I say. Lift your *foot*, tell your slipper.

And my mother totters on, an old shell without a mast, no one knows how she doesn't give in to the abyss.

– Where are we going? asks broken old Eurydice. – Onto the balcony, I say. I can already see your armchair waiting for you. – Good. We are going to the land where language has not yet germinated. As we walk, we continue the sacred conversation.

MY MOTHER. – And now what do I do?

ME. – You lift the other foot. And the slipper shuts up.

MY MOTHER. – I am too old. *(She looks at her foot, but it's the slipper which refuses to budge.)*

ME. – The foot. Not the slipper.

THE SLIPPER. – No, no, no.

MY MOTHER. – Who is this fool? It's not me. *(The slipper resists. The foot is lost. I lift it. I ask my mother to help. The slipper grumpy. Begrudgingly gives in. My mother delighted!)* Alley oop! I didn't use to be like this.

ME. – *(asking the question one must not ask).* – Do you remember? Do you think about how you *used to be*?

MY MOTHER *(opening her eyes wide).* – About me? It's the wildest question she has ever heard! *Me?* At my age, what a question! That's the past. Me, I'm the past.

165

ME. – You don't think about the past? (which you used to think about in the old days when you were still a girl in England, or when you made love with my father, never over-doing it, and in the normal positions, or when, as a midwife, you sped at night toward another woman in labor, I was thinking.)

MY MOTHER. – No! No! *(She laughs.)* What would be the point? The Past – is past. And now where are you taking me?

Now there's a big, necessary, confident question. Calm reigns. My mother looks at the world, she doesn't think about it, she takes note of it. She thinks: my daughter's back is the edge of the world.

Old Eurydice beyond all past.

Alas I tell myself, how far from me, the age of the present without past and without future. The past is not past, nor the past, nor coming back like a ghost from the dead, it remains, threatening, wan, weighted with pain. I can't escape it: where would I go? I can run as fast as I like, I still have O. inside me. I am consumed by O. Now that O. has left, he consumes me. I think of him each time I stop writing. Also each time I begin to write, I must first take a turn around the rock, also each time I fall into a sentence that imprisons me in its knots, the thought of O. stalks me, I note that I think I see a number of words in O., but perhaps this is self-persecution.

I'm going to call him, I say. But right away someone, I don't know who, shouts: to do what? He is going to call. Precisely, I say. I can't stand not calling him myself. I can't stop thinking about calling O., either to satisfy my desire, or to satisfy my fear. Instead of writing. I intercede now in one direction now the other. I spend the day in search of a solution. My dreams side with indecision. O. never turns up in them. I see the world without O. I see the whole world save O. All the same it would help if I knew what I would really like not to say to him. This morning, my mind was made up. Settled. I'm going to call him. Immediately I had a tremendous sense of relief. I'm going to write one page of *Twists and Turns*, it is dawn, and right after I'll call O., I was thinking. This page will give me the courage and the ground from which to spring toward O. But at the mere idea that I was going to call O., the page upon which I had written a forceful, commanding, propulsive opening sentence that promised to take me without detour to my Tower fell flat, breaking, scattered into ten ink-splattered pagelets and all in a wink of an eye.

I must first write and then telephone, I thought, but already this thought sat heavily in front of the writing porch, already the day had tripped up, I'm wrong, I said, one must first telephone, this is obvious, so long as I haven't called O. I will be thinking about telephoning, I will be forever half about to get up and do it, half sitting back down to write to prepare myself to telephone, there'll be a telephone blocking the road, naturally I will be thinking: let's call O., instead of writing I will think about not telephoning, I will be engaged in an arm-wrestling contest and I can only lose, I vacillated, wisdom dictates, I told myself, and I divided myself. My pages reflected and divided themselves in my image, a waste, an inflation of barred, wasted pages, an avalanche of sheets, hundreds of them, scratched out, crumpled-up balls of paper, lifeless masks, twisted, grimacing, dozens of amputated paragraphs. There was a storm. Sheets of white fire unrolled their prodigious specters followed by a cortège of rain drumming on the black ground atremble with sky. The powers were at work. All the species paraded light years into the cosmos. And me, no earthly good. Stuck between two rival vital functions. What could be more simple, I told myself. Shake a leg! Don't let your slipper order you around. I *experience the difficulty*: what my mother must *overcome* within herself in order to overcome a centimeter without. Beginning with lassitude's incessant orders: let it go, give up.

167

At the end of this nanotitanic inner battle, evening falls: one has been pinned in the positions of the morning like a naturalized butterfly. What has changed is the weight. Now one lies under the rubble and in the ruins. Decomposition is about to begin, I tell myself. I am so deeply buried that I abandon all suffering. The memory of the book I was going to write, that I would called *Twists and Turns*, burns low, a poor flame resigned to ash.

I look at my mother. The eyes at the helm. All by themselves they are her face. She can still be my shelter, my old detritus, I can still lay my head on her breast, receive on my skull the awkward, dry little taps she bestows in lieu of caresses, be rocked by the ritual words that bring each day's holy conversation to an end: "I've done nothing today but eat and be. Yes yes yes. Now I'm going to sleep. Time goes by. It's that dial over there that goes round and round. Nothing to be done. Don't get up too early. You've got time. Yes yes yes." And I say yes, yes for yes.

I was looking at my mother, the shadow of the dying day lengthening ahead of me. Suddenly, something happens, something doesn't come, something else slowly emerges. On the face crumpled by the inner blasts, minuscule weak little tears had trickled into the gauzy wrinkles of skin that constitute the peels of her eyelids, for at her age she has nothing left to weep with, the tears too are dehydrated. Reclining on her boat ready to depart for the undiscovered country, daubs of white Kleenex balled up into flakes surrounding her body: this is the tableau. I said: "Mama! Wait!" She distinctly said: "I am miserable." A big flake of Kleenex, a lump of hail, rolled from her right hand. The entire length of her boat strewn with it. Crystallized tear lumps in the corners of her eyes. One is struck by the amplitude of the mute manifestation.

And already I was a mother who knew all that misery was, breathlessly, going to tell me. In a rush it all came out, sharp trembling little blows that she gave me on the arms, on the hands, on the cheeks, and that I forced myself to take without flinching. "I am miserable because O. left, because he said he wanted to leave, because he didn't say what he was thinking, because he didn't want to leave."

I telephoned O. I dialed the number without getting it wrong, I was thinking "only by the salt of violence can we savor the taste of peace."

Translator's Notes

These notes, chapter by chapter, signal some of the subtleties, lost in translation, of the original French text.

AUTHOR'S PREFACE

hateloved (p. vii): in French, *haïmé*, a word invented by joining *haïr*, "to hate," to *aimer*, "to love."

O. ANNOUNCES THE MURDER

I held my mother in my arms, like life itself . . . it is so frail (p. 3): throughout this passage "it" translates the feminine pronoun *elle*, which might refer to the mother, life (*la vie*) and the sentence (*la phrase*), an ambiguity the translator has not been able to capture in English.

we have set sail (p. 3): *on fait voile* (sail, veil) in French.

The sun is shining, but **(p. 6)**: in English in the text. The following mention, however, is in French.

stuck in the ice (p. 6): in French *immobilisés par les glaces*, which might also mean "immobilized by the mirrors."

"I am not in my skin" (p. 8): in French there are many expressions to do with skin that might come to mind here – for instance, *être bien/mal dans sa peau* (to feel good/ill at ease about oneself) – and add to the strange twist that the author has given this almost-familiar statement.

its sluggishness (p. 12): throughout this passage, the pronoun *il* could be translated by "it/its" (the bull/dog) or by "he/his" (O.)

naveer toward the house (p. 14): in French *navirons vers la maison*. In *navirons* one hears both *naviguer* (navigate) and *virer* (veer, turn).

Sleep, it's funny. You can write it differently (p. 18): Here the text plays on the mother's discovery of the homophony between *dort* (sleep) and *d'or* (of gold).

TURNSTILE – *HOPING WITHOUT HOPE*

do you believe that this what there? (p. 27): the French text plays on the sounds of *quoi* (what) and *croit* (believe), as well as on internal rhyme.

I think about my mother. I think about the writing (p. 28): this use of *écriture* allows HC to use the feminine pronoun "her" ambiguously, for both the writing and the mother.

171

"en italiennes" (p. 28): Montaigne writes in the diary of his Italian travels: *elles y reposaient paresseusement, en Italiennes* . . . . ("they were resting, idly in the fashion of Italian women . . . ."); in the French theater one may rehearse "à l'italienne": that is, actors seated, saying their lines, without any dramatic action. HC thought she was referring to the theater here, but was no longer sure (2012).

I aspired, I hoped, I expired (p. 33): in French *J'aspirais, j'espérais, j'espirais.*

THE OTHER COLD

bruising-blue (p. 37): in French *bleuissures*, evoking *bleu* (the color blue, but also a bruise) and *blessure* (wound).

one screeks (p. 42): in French *on crisses*, in which one hears the sound of boots crunching over dry snow but also *on cri* ("one screams").

Whywhywhywhy (p. 43): in French *Pourquoipourquoi?* The translator's problem here is not unlike that of the French translator of *Macbeth*, faced with the line "Tomorrow and tomorrow and tomorrow" (*Demain et demain et demain* gives the literal meaning but loses the feeling of interminability inherent in Shakespeare's line). Cixous's sentence *Pourquoipourquoi?* is literally "Whywhy?" but it is also four syllables long. Two more "why's" have been added to "drag out" the sentence and its time.

why why (p. 43): in French *pourquoi* is spelled *pourcoi* here.

de-rails (p. 53): *dé-raille* in French playing on *railler* ("to mock") and *dérailler* ("to derail" or, familiarly, "to rave")

poo poo poo (p. 54): in French a louse is a *pou* (plural *poux*) and here they shout *pou pou pou*; and, further down, a mad person is *fou*, which rhymes with – dances with – *pou*.

nude humor (p. 54): in French *humour nu*, very close in sound to the more usual and expected *humour noir*, black humor, and which also rhymes with *pou* and *fou*.

THE FAMILY IS DESTROYING ITSELF

I examined it every which way, I built my Tower (p. 57): in fact, what HC writes is ["I already wrote the next chapter...] *j'en ai fait le tour*, which means, literally, "I made the tower," but which is also an idiomatic expression signifying "I examined the problem from every direction."

hateloved (p. 66): in French, as noted in the "Author's Preface," where this passage first appears, *on est haimé*, from *haïr*, "to hate" and *aimer*, "to love."

***The Gold Rush* (p. 66):** in French *La Ruée ver l'or. L'or* (gold) rhymes with *mort* (death, the dead body).

I have *en vie* of death (p. 67): this is a play on the French *envie*, which can mean "to envy," but also, in the phrase *j'ai envie*, "I want, wish, have the desire to." *En vie*, however, spelled as two words, means "in life, living." As this passage continues, it plays more and more on the different ways of reading these syllables.

in front of my desires (p. 67): in French *devant mes voeux*, which echoes the more usual French phrase *devant mes yeux*, "before my eyes."

173

One has done as one *Wished* (p. 68): *On a fait ce dont on avait Envie.* Here English can no longer stay close enough to the French to capture all the plays on the word *Envie*.

SAME SONG DIFFERENT PLAY

the bit, the death (p.77): in French *le mors, la mort.*

the blood of Truth: you are one, you yourself tear yourself apart (p. 77): in French *en sang de la Vérité: elle est une, elle se déchire elle-même* [translation of *elle* (la Vérité) by "you" suggested by HC, April 2012].

the voice of the soul (p. 79): in French "ass" (*âne*) and "soul" (*âme*) look and sound much alike.

the Truth (p. 81): *la Vérité*, which is feminine in French.

calculation (p. 83): *le calcul*, which is masculine in French, leading to some ambiguity later in this paragraph around the masculine pronoun "il," which can refer to both the Archduke and to *le calcul*, personified.

under falling ice (p. 83): in French *coup de glace*, which sounds very much like *coup de grace*.

like a thief, off it flits (p. 83): *comme un voleur, comme un volant*, words with many possible meanings and related sounds, rooted in *voler* ("to steal" but also "to fly"). I have chosen to translate the sound elements of the words, rather than settle for a meaning which will never fully express the semantic charge of the phrases in French.

the forgetbook (p. 93): *l'oublivre.*

"Puscule!" (p. 100): in French the word that the mother has on the tip of her tongue is *crépuscule* ("dusk, twilight"). Chopped up, it gives *cre* + *puce* ("a flea"), which stings, + *cule*, in which she possibly hears *queue* or *cul* ("tail"/"prick"). So the "riddle," syllable by syllable, goes *"Quand le so so le soleil n'est pas encore cou cou couché, il y a juste la puce qui sort et cule aussi qui sort, cule c'est mal élevé et la puce qui pique et pique."*

"There won't be a war," ... **there she is (p. 101):** in French *la guerre* is feminine and personified.

wormy (p. 104): note that the French words for "wormy" (*véreuse*) and "truth" (*vérité*) begin with the same syllable.

hard-of-hearing (p. 104): in French *malentendu* ("misunderstood") means literally "badly heard," and a *malentendant* is a deaf person, so Cixous is playing here on two senses of the word, sliding from one to the other.

MY RIGHT ARM HURTS

to tear it up, let it go (p. 105): in French *le déchirer ou le déchérir*. *Déchérir* is a neologism constructed from *dé* and *chérir*, "to cherish."

beside myself (p. 106): *hors de moi*. HC is, not for the first time, playing on this French idiom, which means literally "outside of myself/my house," but figuratively "beside myself, infuriated."

we looked at we (p. 115): in French *nous regardions nous*, a play on the more usual reflexive *nous nous regardions*. That the French *nous* is at once a subjective, objective and reflexive pronoun allows a subtle slippage of meaning here, which would be lost if this phrase were translated by "we looked at each other (= *nous nous regardions*)," "we looked at us," or even " we looked at ourselves." This slippage or crack in terrain remains present throughout this passage. And the translation is unsatisfactory.

we-ing (p. 115): *nounoyer*, perhaps a compression of *nous* and *noyer* ("to drown"), but also an echo of *vouvoyer*, to use the formal *vous*, as opposed to *tutoyer*, to use the intimate *tu*. There is a further echo of the comforting childhood words *nounou*, "nanny," and *nounours*, "teddy bear."

nourishing (p. 115): *nourir*, in which one hears again the pronoun *nous* (and also *rire*, to laugh).

we'llnotgoagain (p. 116): *nounironplus*, echoing all the above uses of *nous*.

a notgo (p. 116): *un naller*.

And all these masculines (p. 118): *bois* and *lauriers* are masculine nouns in French.

to which nothing ill could happen, or evil, or explosive, or male, she's it. The Castle burned, which is to be expected, but not the Tower (p. 122): In French "ill" is *mal* and "male" is *mâle*; *château* is masculine, but *tour* ("tower") is feminine, and "she" therefore conflates mother and tower, here and below.

the friendship-of-which-I-speak (p. 123): *l'amitié-dequoy-je-parle*. Here and elsewhere in this paragraph Cixous employs a phrase from Montaigne's *Essays* Book I:28, "On Friendship," in which he speaks of his friendship with Étienne de La Boétie:

> *Au demeurant, ce que nous appelons ordinairement amis et amitiés, ce ne sont qu'accointances et familiarités nouées par quelque occasion ou commodité, par le moyen de laquelle nos âmes s'entretiennent. En* l'amitié dequoy je parle, *elles se mêlent et confondent l'une en l'autre, d'un mélange si universel, qu'elles effacent et ne retrouvent plus la couture qui les a jointes. Si on me presse de dire pourquoi je l'aimais, je sens que cela ne se peut exprimer qu'en répondant : "parce que c'était lui ; parce que c'était moi."*

What we usually call friends and friendship are but the acquaintances and familiars brought together by some occasion or convenience, by whose means our souls converse. In *the friendship of which I speak*, they mingle so that you cannot tell them apart, in a mixture so universal that they efface forever the seam that has joined them. If one pressed me to say why I loved him, I sense that I could only respond: "because it was him; because it was me."

"*traveller*," (p. 127): in English in the text.

no trip, no tower, no return to the tower (p. 127): in French "pas de tour, pas de retour. . .". *Tour* in French can mean "trip," "turn" and "tower," and has no equivalent in English. It is a common word and recurs frequently in different contexts, but implicit in them all is perhaps Montaigne's tower and all it has represented in Cixous's books.

Death ... how she (p. 133): "death" (*la mort*) is feminine in French. It could followed by the neutral pronoun "it" in English, but there is a play on its gender here.

save the tie **(p. 134):** *sauver la fisselle. Fisselle*, which doesn't exist, except in the seventeenth-century form *fisele*, is a word which suggests many things: a small wicker basket (now *faisselle*, and often made of pottery, a kind of small colander) used for draining whey from curd in the cheese-making process, but also *ficelle*, "string" or "thread," a word in which one hears *fils*, "son."

"Vor dem Gesetz" (p. 136): "Before the Law," a parable Kafka incorporated into *The Trial*. "Before the Law," which was published during Kafka's lifetime, whereas *The Trial* was not, has also been alluded to and commented on by Jacques Derrida and J.M. Coetzee.

His personal door ... she (p. 138): door is feminine in French, and here we also look back to the gatekeeper at Montaigne.

I entered the Tower *for the first time* in my long history of towers (p. 140): the first tower is Montaigne's; but the second (*tours*) could mean many other things besides, including "turns" and "tricks."

I see the cat that wants to play (p. 142): "When I play with my cat, who knows whether she is not playing with me rather than I with her?" (Montaigne, "In Defense of Raymond Sebond").

We are going to do some chardining (p. 148): a wordplay on the French *jardinier* ("to garden") and the name of the (mostly) still life painter, Chardin.

lout (p. 150): in fact *malautruis*, a word formed from *mal* and *autrui* ("others"), but which sounds like *malotrus*, a boor, an uncivil person. In French the first of the two preceding sentences begins with *L'autre*, which is then echoed by *L'autrui*, followed by *Le malautrui*, so three short sentences in a row hammer on the same word. "Lout," possibly of Germanic origin, sounds like *l'autre*.

fate's scissors (p. 153): *les ciseaux du sort*, which could be translated also as "she would go on holding the scissors in this way . . . ."

no saint without dragon at its breast (p. 154): in French these two words, *saint* and *sein*, sound alike.

It had already gone off (p. 155): in French "it" is *il*, which could also mean "he," that is, O.

TWISTS AND TURNS

"the origin" of the work of art (p. 159): echoes the title of a Heidegger essay, which discusses Van Gogh's painting of a pair of shoes.

we'll have been able to see the narrator's Françoise pluck the asparagus (p. 159): a scene from Proust's *In Search of Lost Time*, in which Françoise is the family servant. In France it is, or once was, usual to eat white asparagus, and to peel the stalks before cooking them.

Now I show her the *Asparagus* again (p. 161): Manet made two asparagus paintings, the first a bunch of asparagus, and the second a single stalk lying diagonally on what appears to be a marble-topped surface.

a port . . . a door (p. 163): in French *port . . . porte.*